MURDER
in MANTEO

MURDER
in MANTEO

Seeking Justice
for Stacey Stanton

JOHN RAILEY

THE
History
PRESS

Published by The History Press
Charleston, SC
www.historypress.com

Front cover, inset: Stacey Stanton's high school graduation portrait; *bottom*: Sir
Walter Raleigh Street in Manteo.
Back cover: Stacey and her cat, Molly.

First published 2024

Manufactured in the United States

ISBN 9781467155700

Library of Congress Control Number: 2024930885

For Stacey and E.
And for Kathleen

The wicked flee when no man pursueth: but the righteous are bold as a lion.
—Proverbs 28:1

CONTENTS

CONTENTS

Author's Note

For decades, young women have been coming in growing numbers to the Outer Banks to work. One of them, Elizabeth Stacey Stanton, twenty-eight, a beloved resident of Manteo, was found dead in her downtown apartment on the Saturday afternoon of February 3, 1990. Her neck, right breast and vagina had been brutally slashed, the most horrendous crime in the town since 1967. A rushed investigation, with the tourist season coming on and the Manteo police chief tangling with his governing board, culminated in a rushed charge and conviction. The questions about Stacey's case linger to this day. Two determined lawyers, one who risked his burgeoning law practice in Manteo and, later, another, who had given up her lucrative corporate career to fight for criminal justice in general, sought to answer those questions.

Stacey could have been their sister or daughter, a realization that never left the lawyers as they worked the case, having to study her crime scene photos that would forever haunt them. She could have been *your* sister. Or *your* daughter. She waited tables in Manteo, charming her patrons with big smiles that belied growing trouble she was experiencing. Even on a tiny island, there are people we think we know but really do not.

In writing this book, I drew from the confidential SBI file on the case, hundreds of my own interviews with lawyers, a key suspect and island insiders. Each interview peeled away another layer toward uncovering the hidden truth, often tied to the complexities of race: Stacey was white, and a main suspect was Black.

Most of the dialogue in this book comes verbatim from the sources mentioned. Other dialogue, including that from SBI interviews, has been recreated based on those sources.

The names Cathy Rogers, Rick Willis, Marty Madden and Sherry Collins are pseudonyms to protect privacy. All other names are real.

It might be easy to dismiss the wrongdoings that will unroll here as something from another era. But the same problems persist to this day nationwide: investigators and prosecutors rushing to make murder charges, leaving the real killers free, endangering the public. Very few law enforcement officers, as in this case, ever admit they erred.

John Railey
Manteo, North Carolina
May 2024

Cast of Characters

The Victim

Elizabeth Stacey Stanton

The Key Investigators

Dennis Honeycutt, State Bureau of Investigation (SBI) agent
Kent Inscoe, SBI agent
Steve Day, Manteo police chief
Jasper Williams, Dare County lieutenant colonel
Tony Cummings, SBI agent

The Prime Suspects

Norman Judson "Mike" Brandon Jr.
Clifton Eugene Spencer

The Prosecutors

District Attorney H.P. Williams and his successor, District Attorney
    Frank Parrish
Assistant District Attorneys Robert Trivette and Amber Davis

CAST OF CHARACTERS

The Defense Lawyers

Romallus Murphy
Edgar Barnes
Letitia Echols
Chris Mumma

Stacey's Parents

Maryanne and Ed Stanton Sr.

PROLOGUE

The Southern Piedmont of North Carolina,
April 24, 2023

Late afternoon, the sun slowly sinking through the tall pines, mourning doves starting to coo in the cool air. A lawyer and I have come unannounced to this house out in the woods. We get out of the car, walk softly across a carpet of pine needles and approach the door. I see a hand push aside the curtain at a front window, and a face briefly appears.

That's her, I whisper to the lawyer. She nods.

We walk up the creaky wooden steps and knock on the door. We wait. It seems like ten minutes, but it's really only a minute. That's the way it is when you're on an old case chase. You spend hundreds of hours alone with a beat-up file, highlighting names, then getting on your laptop, trying to find those names that you're imagining as real people, realizing you might be bringing preconceived notions. You're so anxious to get out and chase the leads.

Many times, you never find the people behind the names on the pages. Other times, you find them, and they meet your original impressions. And sometimes when you find them, they blow your mind and your initial conceptions of the case.

The face in the window opens the door and steps outside. She listens cautiously as the lawyer and I explain our mission: We want to talk to her about the Stacey Stanton case. She is guarded but civil, slowly becoming a bit more welcoming as we talk, occasionally laughing wryly with me as I remind her of shared bar talk on the Outer Banks. We talk about Stacey's case.

This woman dressed in casual clothes is worn but has eyes as blue as the sea on a calm day off Nags Head. Her eyes lighten at times as we talk and flash at other points. She knows things about the night Stacey was killed. We listen. Three decades ago, she reveled in life on Roanoke Island, where she grew up. Now, if she wants seafood, she has to get it from some chain restaurant out on the noisy bypass serving frozen retreads. She is hesitant to talk about the case but glad to talk about the island she loved so far from this place she is now.

Finally, she breaks her long silence, one of many voices encouraging me on in this story.

PART I

THE CRIME

—⁄⁄⁄—

MANTEO, FEBRUARY 3, 1990

1

A TENSE CHRISTMAS

Northfield, New Jersey, Christmas 1989

Stacey looked bummed out, like she didn't want to leave Northfield.
—Ed Stanton Jr., in an interview with the author, April 2023

Ed Stanton Sr., a large and charming operator of a prosperous plumbing company he had started, did not want his daughter Stacey to return to Manteo after Christmas in 1989. Ed and his wife, Maryanne, were both close to Stacey, Ed especially so.

Stacey had made a holiday trip to the house in which she was raised, a comfortable split-level, and was there for the Christmas holidays, always a special time for her family and their close-knit set of friends in their small town in South Jersey, nestled between rolling farmland and just a few minutes' drive from Ocean City and Atlantic City, the beaches Stacey had grown up loving. Northfield calls itself "The Gateway to the Shore."

Stacey, born just before Thanksgiving, on November 16, 1961, was raised in the Catholic Church in Northfield, attending Catholic school, taking her first communion when she was about eight, wearing the traditional white dress of innocence. Stacey, with two older sisters and a younger brother, Ed Jr., was vivacious, fun and smart, full of life.

"She was always such a beautiful girl inside and out and she had a wonderful sense of humor," said one of her Catholic school classmates, Elisa Jo Eagan. Mary Powers, a cousin of Stacey's, agreed.

Another cousin, Cathy Groves, said Stacey had "amazing blue eyes" and a cool style. She was fine-featured, Groves said, with a gorgeous skin tone somewhere between ivory and olive that "just glowed."

Stacey later entered public school, Mainland Regional High School. She was a cheerleader. On weekends, she and her friends hung out at a local mall. Stacey generally stayed out of trouble but was caught smoking pot as a senior in 1980, at a time when many of her contemporaries were smoking. A

Above: Stacey's childhood friend Elisa Jo Eagan (*left*) and Stacey's sister-in-law Sharon Stanton in April 2023. *Kathleen Railey.*

Opposite: Stacey and her brother, Ed. *The Stanton family.*

teacher caught Stacey, and no criminal charge resulted. She graduated from Mainland in June 1980.

After high school, she enrolled in a cosmetology school and waited tables. She was good at haircutting and waitressing. She could also be mischievous. One day, when she told her mother she'd be in school, Stacey skipped class to go to Ocean City. Sometime after, she was caught in an Ocean City postcard on that day sunbathing at the beach. Busted. The family often teased her about that.

Stacey in elementary school. *The Stanton family.*

She dated a local man. They broke up. Stacey's interest turned to the Outer Banks of North Carolina. Her family had struck up a long friendship with Boyd Midgett of Manteo and his family when Midgett had worked in New Jersey for the Atlantic City Electric company in the Northfield area and met Stacey's father. When the Midgetts moved back to Manteo several years before, the Stantons often visited them there.

Stacey struck up a relationship with a Manteo man. In the mid-1980s, Stacey moved to Manteo, on Roanoke Island, to date that man.

Like generations before her, Stacey came to the Outer Banks to make a new start. You can see her making the long drive from Jersey, her belongings packed in the 1976 Ford Granada she'd gotten from an uncle, maybe singing along to the southern rock she loved on her car radio and letting out a yell as she crossed the big suspension bridge high over the Delaware River, ghostly mist rising off the big rolling river far below. She left Jersey behind and rolled on the interstate through Delaware, Maryland and Virginia and finally into North Carolina. After an hour riding south across North Carolina, Stacey finally drove onto the bridge over the shimmering Currituck Sound, the northern entrance to the Outer Banks. There is mind-blowing water stretching for miles on either side until it kisses the sky at the horizon. Seagulls divebomb for fish jumping in the shimmering water, grabbing their prey and then rapidly soaring skyward with catches tight in their beaks. Clouds climb over wooded shorelines pocked by docks.

Stacey exited the bridge, on into Kitty Hawk and Dare County, leaving behind the mainland and old ways.

The Dare name would have resonated with Stacey, who had known it since childhood. The county formed in 1870 is named for Virginia Dare, the first child born of English parents in America, a milestone featured in *The Lost Colony* outdoor drama on Roanoke Island in the summer. But maybe even more than that, the provocative nature of the word *dare* might have hit Stacey. The county had been all about, since its inception, taking dangerous chances. There was the colony that had vanished in the late 1500s. And the county was home to descendants of those who'd shipwrecked off its shores, as well as modern-day outcasts, adrift from family, responsibilities, big cities and other problems. Some came to Dare to find themselves. Others came to lose themselves. It was a place of both forgiveness and foreboding.

Stacey rode down the two-lane Beach Road through the towns of Kitty Hawk, Kill Devil Hills and Nags Head, finally crossing the bridge over the Roanoke Sound to Roanoke Island. The island she'd known since childhood would be hers for the first time as a grown-up.

Boyd Midgett shepherded Stacey. He introduced her to his relatives Sam and Mary Midgett, who leased her a second-floor apartment in a neat brick building on quiet Ananias Dare Street in Manteo for about $300 a month, $700 in 2023 dollars, but still cheap for downtown Manteo, where apartment rents today run well over $1,000 monthly, if you are lucky enough to find an apartment. Sam Midgett was a former Manteo mayor. He and his wife lived in a brick house in front of Stacey's apartment building. Mary's daughter, Nancy Austin, lived in a frame house with her family on the other side of the parking lot in front of the apartment building.

Several years before, the town, capitalizing on its history and *The Lost Colony* connection, had renamed its core streets for historical figures. Ananias Dare was the husband of Eleanor Dare, the mother of Virginia Dare, whom the county

Another shot of Stacey in elementary school. *The Stanton family.*

celebrates as "the first English child born in the New World"—a slight to all the Native Americans born there for generations before.

The island is an insular locality with residents slow to accept outsiders, especially the ones they call "Yankees." Outer Bankers depend on the tourist trade from northerners but sometimes quietly curse those tourists for the traffic jams they bring. Yet New Jersey was a special place for some locals on Roanoke Island. Ginger Tramontano, the owner of a key locals' hangout in Manteo, the Green Dolphin Pub, was from Jersey.

A few locals identified with Stacey's South Jersey, having worked commercial fishing trips off Cape May. Most important for Stacey was her family's friendship with Boyd Midgett and his family. That connection was her intro. Stacey did the rest by just being herself: blonde, loyal and fun.

Older Roanoke Islanders refer to newcomers as "wash-ins," a phrase hearkening back to the days when survivors of shipwrecks in the "Graveyard of Atlantic," the treacherous shoals off their coast where the cold Labrador Current meets the warm Gulf Stream one, made it ashore. In the early days, those wash-ins settled down and built generations of families on the Outer Banks sand. But in modern history, as bridges replaced ferries, wash-ins drove in. Locals regarded them cautiously, accepting a few as their own. Andy Griffith, who made his home on

Right: Stacey's high school graduation photo, 1980. *The Stanton family.*

Opposite, top: Stacey, in the middle front, next to her brother, Ed, far left, at Ocean City, New Jersey. A cousin stands behind them, and another cousin stands in front of Stacey's mother, Maryanne. *The Stanton family.*

Opposite, bottom: Postcard of Stacey, circled, sunbathing at Ocean City, New Jersey, in the 1980s. *The Stanton family.*

Top: Aerial shot of Manteo a few years before Stacey was slain. *The Outer Banks History Center, State Archives.*

Bottom: Stacey's apartment was on the far right, second floor of the building in the middle of this 2023 photo. *John Railey.*

Sir Walter Raleigh Street, downtown Manteo, a few years before Stacey was killed. The last building on the right housed Fernando's bar and, later, the Green Dolphin. *J. Foster Scott photo via the Outer Banks History Center, State Archives.*

Roanoke Island, is the most notable example, having made his start in *The Lost Colony* generations before.

Stacey was a long way from being as accepted as Andy. But she was getting there.

The walls of Stacey's apartment were painted white. She bought an aquarium and stocked it with her favorite fish. She added to her refrigerator a photo of her hugging her father and pasted some words above it: "Stacey's on my side." Their twin grins jumped out at you.

She cut hair and landed a job waiting tables at the Duchess of Dare restaurant, which everyone called "the diner," in downtown Manteo.

For her hairdressing, she first worked for Donetta Livesay at her salon in downtown Manteo. "She was a good employee and always professional, no problems ever," Donetta said. "No small talk from her, just there to do her job, which she did well. She was quite an attractive girl, but never brought attention to herself. She was a mystery, not in a bad way, just how she maneuvered herself. She was to herself and a quiet introvert."

The Duchess of Dare diner, where Stacey worked. *The Outer Banks History Center, State Archives.*

Walker's Diner in Manteo, which later became the Duchess of Dare diner. *Outer Banks History Center, State Archives.*

Doris Walker, Stacey's boss at the Duchess of Dare restaurant in Manteo. *Earlene Sawyer.*

Stacey welcomed Blacks to her home, more so than many of her fellow islanders.

She was slender, five feet, five inches tall and 116 pounds, moving easily among her many island friends. Yolanda "Yoyo" Daniels, who lived on Devon Street, one street over from Stacey, met her as Yoyo walked her toddlers in the neighborhood. They soon became friends, with Stacey occasionally babysitting Yoyo's children, and doing it well, Yoyo said. "She was so sweet," Yoyo added, remembering that Stacey bought her daughter a doll that she treasured for years.

Stacey began cutting hair from her apartment while still waiting tables at the diner. The restaurant was just one street over from her home. The restaurant had begun as Walker's Diner decades before. Later, as the town embraced its Elizabethan heritage, the owners added a Tudor façade and changed the name to Duchess of Dare. Locals kept pouring in, loving the local seafood, the hush puppies and the bread and rice puddings.

The tips were good for Stacey. She worked hard and seemed happy, even bubbly on some days. Her employers—Doris Walker, the matriarch, nicknamed "the Duchess," and her son Carl, nicknamed "Tom Thumb," and his sisters Carol and Earlene—loved her, and so did the regulars. Many Roanoke Islanders and their friends on the nearby beaches had for years been nicknamed: "Punk," "Gov," "Winkie," "Possum," "Trapper," "Bad Boy," "Buster," "Zero," "Buck" and "Sleeper" being just a few.

Commercial fishermen, lawyers, local politicians, and retirees gathered at a spot in the restaurant called the "Round Table," eating, smoking, drinking coffee and swapping stories.

The regulars loved talking with Stacey. Between the tips and cutting hair, Stacey was making it.

Her little brother, Ed Jr., a plumber carrying on his father's business, always close to Stacey and three years younger than her, visited her in Manteo twice, staying in her apartment. They partied and talked about their growing-up days, including family ski trips to Rutland, Vermont. "She was my best friend," Ed said. "She got along with everybody. She was a loving, caring person."

Near the diner was the old brick courthouse with its whitewashed pillars, rebuilt in 1904 and within sight of Shallowbag Bay, with its adjoining jail behind it, the source of many of the Round Table stories. The courthouse also housed the Dare County Sheriff's Office. The courthouse was full of characters, including Dotty Fry, the register of deeds, a former model who told wonderful stories as she chain-smoked Virginia Slims, charming all with her sparkling blue eyes as she sat back and crossed her long legs.

On her days off, Stacey rode over the Roanoke Sound bridge to the Nags Head beach, cranking up southern rock hits such as Lynyrd Skynyrd's "Sweet Home Alabama" on her car radio and singing along, joining a caravan of

The Duchess of Dare diner was a favorite gathering for Manteo locals. In this shot from the early 1990s, former Manteo police chief Ken Whittington danced across a tabletop to confront photojournalist Drew Wilson. *Drew C. Wilson/the* Virginian-Pilot.

The old Manteo courthouse in downtown Manteo. *John Railey.*

tired old men in convertibles, fight-ready boys in jacked-up trucks with Confederate flags flapping from their antennas and cars packed with gaping children and happy dogs hanging their smiling heads out the windows. Sometimes the other vehicles sported license plates from her native Jersey and adjacent Pennsylvania that would make Stacey grin. She would park at Jennette's Pier and walk across a small dune to the beach, setting up her chair and lounging, just like back in South Jersey but only better on the less-crowded Nags Head beach, watching that wild and wonderful sea.

Ed Stanton Sr. had met many of the locals through Boyd Midgett. They partied together when the Stanton family visited the Outer Banks and hit the locals' favorite restaurants, including Owens' in Nags Head. Both were leaders in their communities, Midgett having been so in South Jersey, then taking on a similar role when he returned to his home island, winning election to the Manteo Board of Commissioners.

That Christmas of 1989, the family saw that something was bothering Stacey, usually so fun. In early January, the Stantons hosted a family dinner at their house. Everybody was happy to see Stacey, including her paternal grandmother, Eleanor Stanton, who thought Stacey "set the moon and the stars." But cousin Cathy Groves noted that Stacey "wasn't herself. There was something off about her," Groves said.

She said Stacey talked about getting back to her boyfriend in Manteo, Norman Judson "Mike" Brandon Jr. She wore heavy makeup, which was not like her, Groves said, and their grandmother speculated that it was to cover earlier bruises from a possible beating.

Family members noticed that Ed Sr. and Stacey gathered in quiet talks over the holidays. She apparently told her father about problems with her boyfriend. She'd wanted Brandon to come with her to Jersey for Christmas, but Brandon declined. Stacey loved Brandon. He was thirty-three, 185 pounds of construction-worker muscle roped over an imposing six-foot, three-inch frame. He had curly brown hair, blue eyes and a way of charming people, especially women, until he got wasted on beer and coke.

Stacey probably didn't tell her father that Brandon had been in trouble with the law since his teenage years and had spent almost half his life in prison for burglary, larceny and other convictions, or that he moved in a shadowy drug subculture in Manteo.

But loving fathers know their daughters. They sense unease in the unspoken.

Ed Stanton loved his children fiercely. He was six feet tall and two hundred pounds but seemed even bigger, with a bushy head of gray hair, and carried himself confidently, an old-school, mustachioed man of the world. He was

Stacey's artwork. *The Stanton family.*

an unofficial godfather in his neighborhood, quietly solving disputes. And he had a gentle side. He was an artist, painting and sketching beach scenes and, on one occasion to honor Boyd Midgett, a caricature of him. Stacey had taken after him, doing her own sketching.

In early January 1990, Stacey loaded up her car to return to Manteo. Her father begged her to stay in Northfield. "He wasn't getting good vibes on what was going on down there," said Stacey's brother, Ed Stanton Jr.

Stacey insisted that she had to return, she had her job and her silver tabby cat, Molly. "Stacey looked bummed out, like she didn't want to leave," Ed Jr. said.

Stacey hugged her father, got in her car and drove off. Ed Sr. sadly watched the taillights vanish. He called Boyd Midgett, telling him to keep an eye on his daughter. Midgett assured his friend he would do so.

2

WHERE'S STACEY?

Manteo, February 2 and February 3, 1990

There was such a quiet order to downtown Manteo, with its happy families living in cute bungalows on quaint streets, but Stacey's own life had become so disordered.

I t was a lazy winter afternoon in Manteo, a Friday, February 2. The town was in the midst of revitalization, having restored much of its beat-up downtown to draw in more tourists. But in winter, the tourists were sparse, with few shops open. A light wind blew from the ocean, over the Roanoke Sound that separates Manteo from Nags Head and the rest of the northern Outer Banks. The wind whispered from the Sound and into Shallowbag Bay, the harbor that elbows around Manteo, the main community of Roanoke Island and the seat of Dare County. The county rolls from Hatteras Island to the south to the Currituck County line near the town of Duck to the north, a beguiling strip of sand between the sounds and the Atlantic Ocean.

Roanoke Island, holding its own between the mainland and the Outer Banks, is but a dot on maps. It is about ten miles long and three miles wide at its thickest points and is bounded on the west by the Croatan Sound, on the east by the Roanoke Sound, on the north by the Albemarle Sound and on the south by the Pamlico Sound. The hedonistic island has always been welcoming and nonjudgmental.

There was a magic to the place, with *The Lost Colony* having four decades before birthed the career of Andy Griffith, who had worked his way up to playing Sir Walter Raleigh in the play. Raleigh had set up the English colony that would be legendarily lost, but never made it there himself.

Now Andy lived in a fine house on the North End of the island. The year before, 1989, he had filmed a double episode of his latest show, *Matlock*, on the island, his way of giving business back to his island. The show, the opener for the series' 1990 season, had dealt with a murder, rare for the island, and drug dealing, not rare at all.

That Friday, it was a mild sixty-five degrees, the damp salt air comfortably cool on local skins. Over on the beach, the partiers were readying for a night out at the bars open in the winter such as Lance's in Nags Head and the Holiday Inn bar in Kill Devil Hills. Manteo partiers would brave DUIs (driving under the influence charges) and go to the beach bars or get a taxi there, but many stuck to their favorite bar in Manteo, the Green Dolphin Pub on Sir Walter Raleigh Street, right in the heart of the small downtown.

The Green Dolphin was fun as hell, with favorite songs like "Red Red Wine" by the band UB40 and Alice Cooper's "School's Out" rocking the jukebox. The clientele included commercial fishermen, bulk-headers, carpenters and waitresses, along with Coast Guard workers, the latter loving their adrenaline-rushed work in one of the country's most challenging spots, the Graveyard of the Atlantic. There were lawyers, politicians, hard workers and pikers, some with "papers" hanging over them, charges for problems ranging from assault to drunken driving. Andy Griffith had filmed one of the *Matlock* scenes in the bar. The pub's offerings include homemade lasagna, she-crab soup and, of course, cold beer.

The building housing the bar had started as a gas station decades before. Many of the current locals had loved the place since its original bar incarnation in the early 1970s, Fernando's. Tempers sometimes ran hot and led to fists thrown, especially around the pool table. It was a battling culture that ran from the island to the beaches across the bridge. One local around that time, drinking in a '57 Chevy outside a beach bar, told a friend, "I'll f—— and I'll fight, but I try not to do both on the same night."

Unlike some of the beach bars, fights usually didn't break out in the Green Dolphin, although they had. As one bulk-header put it, "If we had to fight, we'd usually walk outside and settle it."

The Dolphin was usually packed with characters like Dennis "Den" Midgett, the town's unofficial watchman because of his habit of checking store doors at night to make sure they were locked. He had mental challenges but was sweet as he drank his Budweisers and smoked his cigarettes. Many of the regulars spoke in the Outer Banks brogue, riffing on the Old English of their ancestors, *tide* pronounced "toide" and *ice* pronounced "oice." Politicians stopped by as well, including Marc Basnight of Manteo, on his way to becoming the most powerful leader of the state senate in modern history, charming the Raleigh crowd with his beautiful brogue as he waltzed around them in getting his bills transformed into legislation, millions of dollars in pork-barrel money flowing into Outer Banks projects.

At the Dolphin, especially in the winter, locals gathered and swapped stories. The winter days were long and lonesome, the wind with its brokenhearted roar sweeping across the marshes, mourning doves accentuating the feel when they came on toward sunset, cooing their songs best not listened to by the faint of heart. In Manteo, like other coastal towns the world over, locals gravitated toward the light to greet old friends and meet new ones in bars like the Dolphin, trading old stories and living out new ones. The companionship was important. So was the timeless search for love, something beyond a one-night hookup.

After work, Stacey loved blowing off steam at the Dolphin with her buddy boys and girls. It was all part of the smoky dramedy, easing the workday week, especially on Fridays.

For the most part, Manteo police officers left the Dolphin alone, although several of the customers had run-ins with the law away from the bar. The police department was led by Chief Steve Day, a forty-seven-year-old Coast Guard veteran with a tour of duty in Vietnam who'd retired as a chief warrant officer after thirty years of service. He had been hired as the Manteo chief just five months before, in late August 1989, in part to clean up corruption in the department. While with the Coast Guard, he had worked drug smuggling cases with local law enforcement and earned their respect. Day, who chain-smoked Marlboros, was six feet, four inches tall, with close-cropped gray hair and a direct way of getting his points across. He was known to be fair and honest.

Stacey stopped by the Dolphin early on the night of Friday, February 2. She wore a short pink skirt with blue pinstripes, a mint-green top and tennis shoes. It was not a good night.

Mike Brandon had recently dumped her for a new, younger girlfriend, Patty Rowe, who worked at the Dolphin. They were in the bar that night. Stacey tried to talk to Brandon about reuniting and got nowhere, with Rowe, who was off work, glowering at her. Stacey was twenty-eight, and Patty was in her early twenties.

From across the bar, Stacey saw a friend she and Brandon shared, Clifton Eugene Spencer. Spencer was six-foot-two and 190 pounds, tall and

Manteo police chief Steve Day, one of the lead investigators on Stacey's case. *Drew C. Wilson via the Outer Banks History Center, State Archives.*

handsome. He was separated from his German wife, whom he had met in her native country a few years before while serving in the Air Force. She had custody of their two-year-old daughter, and they had returned to Germany.

Stacey left the bar. Tangled thoughts rolled through her head, and she felt very low. She loved the island and her independence there and didn't want to retreat to Jersey. But she'd fallen into a tough spot. There was such a quiet order to downtown Manteo, with its families living in cute bungalows on quaint streets, but her own life had become so disordered. She put on her happy face every day, serving the customers who loved her at the diner.

But when she left the diner and the Green Dolphin and went back to her small apartment, winter on the island was so damned lonely. She confided in a few friends, yet no one knew the extent of what she was going through.

At her doorway that Friday night, Stacey realized she'd lost her apartment key. Les Austin, a local high school student and one of the landlord's grandchildren who lived in the tan house in front of the apartment building with his parents, used a master key to let Stacey in her apartment. That was the main door that required a key, but it was often unlocked, with just the storm door locked. The storm door had a latch, but visitors often opened it by reaching through a loose pane on the door, releasing the latch and turning the handle.

—⁓—

STACEY ALWAYS SHOWED UP for work on time at the diner.

When she didn't make her 2:00 p.m. shift on Saturday, February 3, 1990, her co-workers worried. Maybe she'd just had a wild night into the early morning and was still sleeping it off, they hoped. Terri Williams, a Dare County deputy sheriff who moonlighted by hostessing at the restaurant, sent a co-worker, waitress Tina Bass, to check on Stacey. Bass came back minutes later, telling Williams that she couldn't get Stacey up and she was lying on her living room floor, with blood near her head. Williams called "central communications," the local equivalent of 911, and went back to the apartment with Bass.

Williams went in the apartment alone and found Stacey lying on her back in her living room, her right arm and shoulder on the back left corner of a blue-and-white-striped bloodstained mattress in front of the switched-off TV, nude except for a light blue long-sleeve shirt pulled up over her breasts. Her head was turned to her left, her eyes were closed and her mouth was

Top: Sir Walter Raleigh Street, downtown Manteo, as Stacey would have seen it on the last night of her life. *J. Foster Scott photo via the Outer Banks History Center, State Archives.*

Bottom: Waitress in the Duchess of Dare diner, where Stacey worked. *Drew C. Wilson via the Outer Banks History Center, State Archives.*

slightly open, revealing her eyeteeth. Her expression was one of subdued anguish. Her arms were behind her head, bent at the elbows, her hands touching a bloodstained pillow on the brown carpet. Her legs were spread, bent at the knees. There were obvious cuts to her throat, right breast and vagina and numerous bloodstains. Williams saw the cut to the breast was deep, exposing the yellow, fatty region, yet there was no blood, which told Williams her friend was dead: her blood had stopped pumping. Williams felt Stacey's wrist and could not get a pulse.

After just a moment, Williams turned to leave the apartment without touching anything. She knew the crime scene should be preserved. As the front door, she met Bass, who was about to come in. In her native Southside Virginia drawl, Williams told Bass that Stacey was dead, and they had to leave. As they left the apartment, other officers and EMTs were arriving.

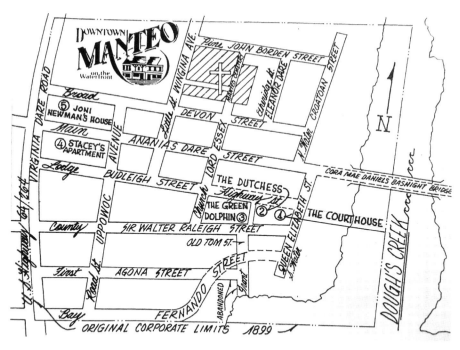

This map of Manteo by former mayor John Wilson IV shows the tight confines of Stacey's case, with her apartment, workplace (the Duchess of Dare) and hangout (the Green Dolphin) all within a few blocks. Also noted on the map is the courthouse and Joni Newman's house, both of which figure heavily in Stacey's story. *John Wilson IV.*

Williams, like other law enforcement workers who responded, would later say she had never come upon such a brutal crime scene, images that would long haunt her and other officers who had known Stacey.

Law enforcement officers and journalists try to forget crimes scenes, usually unsuccessfully. They keep recurring, rattling like old bones through the canyons of our minds. As the great fiction writer Elmore Leonard once wrote, "You get used to the sight of death, but never to expecting it.…An hour later, a week later, a dozen years later, the picture will flash in your memory, vivid, stark naked of hazy forgetfulness."

Lieutenant Colonel Jasper Williams of the Dare County Sheriff's Office (no relation to Terri Williams) soon arrived. A big guy with a mustache, he had been with the sheriff's office since 1976. As the senior officer on the scene, he would later say, he called his boss, Sheriff Bert Austin, and Police Chief Steve Day, who in turn called in the State Bureau of Investigation's (SBI) mobile crime lab. The SBI often helps North Carolina law enforcement agencies with serious cases. The mobile crime lab came from Greenville, North Carolina, about 115 miles west of Manteo.

Lieutenant Colonel Williams would later testify that he "sealed off the crime scene." But Larry Dillon, a Manteo painter who had been scheduled to paint Stacey's place that day, arrived that afternoon to find chaos around her apartment. He walked up the stairs and into her home, finding numerous law enforcement officers and other bystanders. Nobody stopped him or told him to leave, he said.

Deputy Terri Williams went by the apartment later that afternoon, finding it "a zoo," with civilian gawkers walking in and out, going against all she'd learned about securing crime scenes. And that afternoon back at the diner, some of the interlopers were talking loudly about what they'd seen at the crime scene. Williams said she told Lieutenant Colonel Williams that the interlopers should be silenced, but he shrugged her off. Her job was civil justice duties, not criminal justice ones.

Local law enforcement officers called Boyd Midgett, knowing he was close to Stacey's family. Midgett, in turn, called the Stantons' Catholic priest, whom he knew through the family, and asked him to alert them. Monsignor John Clarke quickly went to the Stantons' house. Clarke, in his fifties, was a native of Ireland, silver-haired handsome and beloved in the community. He sat down with Stacey's parents, relaying the terrible news. Stacey's brother, Ed, quickly got the word and raced to his parents' house. Soon, family and friends heard as well. They came to the Stanton

Dare County lieutenant colonel Jasper Williams, one of the lead investigators on Stacey's case. *Drew C. Wilson.*

house with bulging dishes of cold cuts, potato salad, soft pretzels and subs—Jersey comfort food.

The family had not heard from Stacey for a couple of weeks, unusual for her. Her landline phone may have been cut off because Stacey was unable to pay the bill. Cellphones were just starting to catch on, and Stacey didn't have one.

At the home of Stacey's parents, everyone hugged and stood around awkwardly, furious at the unknown killer, lost in their memories of Stacey, staring at their landline phone, hoping it would ring with news from Boyd Midgett.

3

THE CRIME SCENE

By the time the SBI Crime Lab arrived, numerous bystanders had for hours tramped through Stacey's apartment.

S BI agent Dennis Honeycutt and his SBI Crime Lab got to Stacey's apartment from Greenville about 7:25 p.m. that Saturday, almost five and a half hours after Stacey's body had been discovered. Honeycutt wrote in a report that his team had been called in, apparently by Chief Day, about 4:45 p.m. The reason for the delay in calling them is uncertain. The mobile lab could have easily driven the SBI lab in from Greenville in two hours or less.

As it was, by the time the SBI arrived, numerous bystanders had for hours tramped through the apartment. Despite that, Honeycutt simply noted that the stairs leading up to Stacey's second-floor apartment "were roped off to prevent entry."

Honeycutt, a graduate of East Carolina University in Greenville, had joined the SBI in 1982.

The apartment building was at the back of a parking lot/courtyard. In front of the building were the Austin and Midgett houses. There were three apartments in the building in which Stacey had lived: her apartment; another, adjacent to hers, rented by a single man; and, on the floor above her, an apartment rented by Todd Daniels.

A motion light came on as Honeycutt approached Stacey's car, parked outside the apartment building.

In the apartment were empty Busch beer cans, vodka bottles and Marlboro Light cigarette butts, like a party had just ended. Stacey's silence was chilling, her fish still swimming in the aquarium, staring out with their tiny doll's eyes.

Honeycutt noted Stacey's body, lying on its back on a brown carpet between a blue-and-a-white-striped mattress and a TV, right shoulder and arm on the end of the mattress.

"The body was clad only in a blue shirt," Honeycutt wrote. There was a gold chain around her neck, he noted, and she wore "gold-colored earrings."

The jewelry left behind signaled that the killing had not been part of a robbery.

There were blood splatters "on a sheet being utilized as a curtain on the west wall of the den," Honeycutt wrote, above the couch. In the northwest corner of the room, he wrote, he "observed a small plastic table on top of which were also blood splatters. Further, on the east wall of the den near the northeast corner were several other linear blood splatters....On the front of the television within this room which is directly in front of the body of the victim were several more blood spatters."

Honeycutt continued: "It was apparent that numerous stabbings and slashing type wounds were present." He noted that "the arms of the victim

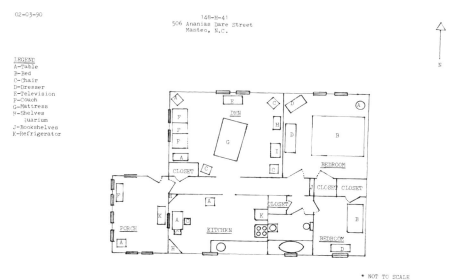

State Bureau of Investigation sketch of the crime scene, Stacey Stanton's Manteo apartment. *SBI.*

were both over her head…with her hands located beneath a pillow…while her legs were spread extremely wide apart and bent at the knees. The only clothing on the victim was a blue thermal-type shirt which was pushed up above the breasts. The shirt was heavily blood stained."

By one side of the body was a pair of bloodstained gray sweatpants turned inside out and a pair of panties.

"The wounds to the body were mostly at the area of the neck with the entire front portion of the neck cut open to the point that SA Honeycutt could see bone," Honeycutt wrote, referring to himself in the third person as he would throughout the report. "Cutting type wounds were also present on the right side of the neck, some of these wounds being superficial. Several superficial cuts were also observed to the area of the top of the chest of the victim."

"A shallow cut to the right breast of the victim was also observed by SA Honeycutt," Honeycutt continued. "This cut was postmortem. Two postmortem cuts were further observed near the area of the vagina. No bleeding was present at this area. Further examination of the body of the victim yielded the finding of transfer-type bloodstains in the following areas: right side of the abdomen, inside the right thigh, inside the left thigh, left calf, right calf."

"Transfer bloodstains" are made when blood from an original source is touched on other areas.

"SA Honeycutt further observed a blood smear on the bottom of the right foot of the victim. Located on the inside of the left thigh of the victim was an area of bruising," Honeycutt wrote. "SA Honeycutt attempted to process the body of the victim for the presence of latent prints, with negative results."

Honeycutt wrote that he "turned over the mattress," and the blood on it "had completely soaked through."

He wrote that he took numerous photos, fingerprint impressions and hair samples. He collected hairs from her body, as well as hairs found in her mouth and clutched in her hands.

Honeycutt wrote that he gathered blood-spattered white lady's tennis shoes near the body. A couch near the body in the living room, he wrote, bore "the presence of small blood spatters near the bottom area.…Blood smears also appear on the northernmost section of the three (3) section couch.…On top of this northernmost cushion was a magazine opened to page 29."

The article displayed in the magazine was headlined "Grey Matter," a story about the actress Jennifer Grey, who'd starred in the 1987 blockbuster *Dirty Dancing*, about a doctor's daughter falling in love with a dance teacher in New York's Catskills in 1963. Key scenes were shot at Lake Lure, in the mountains of North Carolina. The movie was old-school romance, perhaps the kind of which Stacey had dreamed. In real life, Grey was twenty-nine, just a year older than Stacey, and Grey, like Stacey, had waited tables.

"It was further observed that two (2) spatters of blood were present on the open pages," Honeycutt noted.

He also noted that a broken gold necklace containing bloodstains was found on the floor near the couch. "The ring on the clasp of the necklace was forced apart," he wrote.

"Immediately to the right upon walking into the kitchen is a butcher block table on top of which was an empty Busch beer car," Honeycutt wrote. "Immediately beside the beer can, on the table, was an area containing blood staining." He noted that a landline phone in the kitchen was not working. On a kitchen table, he wrote, was Stacey's brown pocketbook with a blue wallet and blue purse. In the purse was a bottle of perfume, an ink pen, a tube of lip balm and Stacey's driver's license. On the stove were two empty two-liter Diet 7-Up bottles and two unopened Busch beer cans. In the refrigerator, he observed, was a bottle of vodka, orange juice and water. In the kitchen trash, he found a paper towel with what appeared to be blood on it, an empty Busch twelve-pack carton and an empty vodka bottle.

In the bathroom, he found more bloodstains, including on a door frame. In the sink area, he wrote, there was "what appeared to be blood" "on the top of the sink and in the basin of the sink. The same type stains were observed on items within the trash immediately below the sink. This area was also photographed and tested for the presence of blood with positive results. SA Honeycutt then processed the sink for the presence of latent prints with no prints of value being noted."

In the hallway of the apartment, above a bookcase, "was an area of bloodstaining," he wrote.

Honeycutt noted that the *Virginian-Pilot* newspaper of that day lay on a chair in the living room. The newspaper was delivered to downtown areas like Stacey's apartment around 6:00 a.m. In the porch area of the house, Honeycutt noted, he found a crack pipe in a dresser drawer. He also noted a letter addressed to Mike Brandon and a receipt from the Food-A-Rama grocery store in Manteo from a couple of days before. Many locals shopped there, giving their business to the locally owned store instead of the Food Lions over on the beach. You can see Stacey wheeling her cart down the aisles of the Food-A-Rama, pausing to gossip with friends.

In the apartment parking lot, investigators gathered a bloody washcloth.

Somewhere around, probably outside, was Stacey's cat, Molly.

Honeycutt's report makes no mention of dismantling the drainpipes of each sink in Stacey's apartment, as well as the shower drain, so that apparently was not done. Those drains might well have included blood, hair or other evidence. The report does not mention an inventory of clothes found in the apartment. The SBI made no mention of checking Stacey's phone records in the days ahead, an investigative basic, especially in those days when phone bills came monthly in print copies

Stacey Stanton and her cat, Molly. *The Stanton family.*

with detailed listings of each call made, its duration and to where the call was made or received.

The apartment walls were thin. A woman who was visiting her boyfriend, Todd Daniels, in the apartment above Stacey's Friday night told the author she heard something that sounded like scuffling that night, but she wasn't sure on the time.

Ray Griggs, who had lived in the apartment beside Stacey's until a few months before her slaying, told the author in a May 2023 email that

> *Stacey Stanton was a great friend and a great person. She was a personality that could speak with anyone. That's probably what made her such a good waitress at the Duchess of Dare restaurant. The ability to speak with anyone. That could be good and bad I guess. If you let the good people into your personal circle, I guess that allows the "not-so-good" folks in as well. I hate to think that her kind, trusting ways could have been her downfall. Because, obviously, whoever did this to her was evil....All I know is, Stacey DID NOT deserve that. It's unfathomable to even think of the horror she must have gone through. Unimaginable. She was my neighbor and friend. We had so many good times and laughs. She was a very positive, upbeat personality. It still makes me shake my head when I think about it....Stacey was an awesome personality and a good friend. A super nice person who would help anyone. I still remember our laughs and conversations. She loved that song by Great White, "Once Bitten, Twice Shy." Every time I hear it, it always reminds me of her. To this day. She may have had flaws, but so does every individual who has ever lived, except Jesus Christ.*

Nancy Austin, who lived in the frame house in front of Stacey's apartment building, told the author in June 2023 that she and her husband went to bed early and did not hear anything that night. They knew Stacey, she said, but not well.

PART II

The Investigation

—⁂—

Manteo, February through May 1990

4
THE LOOK IN THAT GUY'S EYES

I'd never seen him like he was last night.
—Mike Brandon describing Clifton Eugene Spencer on the night Stacey was
killed to investigators

I n the hours before the SBI mobile crime lab arrived, and later, as
the lab worked the crime scene, the investigators were doing their
initial interviews.

Saturday afternoon in his office in the courthouse, Lieutenant Colonel
Williams interviewed Cathy Rogers. He knew she worked at the Green
Dolphin and had asked her to come in for the interview. Rogers was
a smart, hard worker who approached the world with a tough, no-
nonsense style. She brought up the name of Mike Brandon, Stacey's
former boyfriend.

> *Williams: Did you see Stacey yesterday?*
> *Rogers: Yes. Not long after I came to work, she came in and didn't want*
> *anything to drink at first. Later, someone brought her something to drink.*
> *Williams: Did you see anything out of the way, arguments, et cetera?*
> *Rogers: Nothing out of the way except between a Black guy named Cliff*
> *and two Coast Guard boys.*
> *Williams: Did you talk to Stacey?*
> *Rogers: Yes.*
> *Williams: What did you talk about?*

The Green Dolphin Pub in Manteo, where Stacey stopped by hours before she was killed. *County of Dare.*

Rogers: Stacey thought Mike [Brandon] *would leave Patty Rowe* [his new girlfriend]. *She, Stacey, asked me if Patty was pregnant. I told her yes, that she would be foolish to go back to Mike.*

Williams: Did you see Stacey talking to others?

Rogers: To Cliff, the Coast Guard guys, one named Jeff.

Williams: Did you see or hear any arguments?

Rogers: Yes, somebody told Jeff the Coast Guard guy that Spencer took fifty cents off the table. Stacey was in the pool room at the time.

Williams: Do you know anyone else who may have talked to Stacey?

Rogers: Barbara "Bobbi" McGuinness. Cliff, I was told, he went to Stacey's apartment. Mike told us.

Williams: Who is Cliff?

Rogers: Never seen him before last night.

Williams: How long did you talk to Stacey?

Rogers: About five minutes.

Williams: How much did Cliff have to drink?

Rogers: Two to three beers. He was acting weird and rude.

Williams: What do you mean by rude?

Rogers: Trying to pick fights, made remarks [like] *"just a bunch of dumb white folks."*

—‹‹‹—

SATURDAY NIGHT, MIKE BRANDON approached the investigators. In that interview, at 9:40 p.m., he talked to SBI agent Kent Inscoe and Chief Day. Brandon told the lawmen he was Stacey's ex-boyfriend and he'd heard at the Green Dolphin that afternoon about Stacey's death. He was a native of Tarboro, a northeastern North Carolina town about two hours west of Manteo. He'd moved to Manteo several years ago.

Brandon told them:

> *I lived with Stacey until December of last year, when I left and started going with Patty Rowe. Patty is pregnant by me. Yesterday afternoon I got off work about 5:30. My boss dropped me off in downtown Manteo. I walked to the Green Dolphin to meet Patty, who works there and gets off at 5. I got to the bar about 6. Patty was there, drinking beer. Stacey was in the bar, too.*
>
> *I cashed my paycheck at the bar. The bartender took my bar tab from the check and gave me what was left. I bought a beer. I started shooting pool and drinking. Stacey kept making eye contact with me. She came up and asked me how I was doing, and if I was ready to come home.*
>
> *I told Stacey that Patty didn't like the way she was making eyes at me. About 8:30, Stacey came up to me again and started rubbing on me. I told her Patty was there and mad, and it was time for her (Stacey) to go home. Stacey told me she loved me, and I said I loved her. Stacey left between 8:30 and 9. As she was leaving, Bobbi McGuinness started cussing me, telling me I should take Stacey home. Bobbi was upset because Stacey was drunk when she left.*
>
> *Around 10 p.m., a friend of mine, Cliff Spencer, came up to me in the bar. I'd seen him earlier there. He told me he'd just been to Stacey's and she was upset and wanted to talk to me. Cliff said Stacey had said something about killing herself. I told him I couldn't go see Stacey, that Patty was in the bar. Cliff asked me if I wanted some "coke," referring to cocaine. I told him no. He asked me if I would loan him some money for some coke. I told him no.*
>
> *Cliff said, "I'm the only n—— in here and you're acting like the rest of the white boys." He got in an argument with some white boys about some money. I told the bartender to tell Cliff to calm down or leave. Cliff shook my hand and told me he would probably stop by to see Stacey and left. He was broke. He had tried to get me to buy him some beer. That was about 11 p.m. I didn't see Cliff after that.*

Cliff had been at Stacey's several times when I was there. He'd smoked crack five or six times at Stacey's. Me and Stacey also smoked crack with Cliff.

Cliff was broke last night because he tried to get me to buy him some beer. He was trying to pick up a woman. Cliff had brought a white woman to Stacey's apartment once, wanting to use the bedroom. I don't know if Stacey let him. I didn't know the woman.

I knew Cliff through Kellogg Supply. Cliff had been a delivery driver for them, and he would deliver materials to jobs where I was working. Cliff didn't have a car. He hitchhiked around. He had a bike for a while. He stayed with friends in Manteo, sometimes at Stacey's apartment.

Last night, me, Patty, Joni Newman, my sister Tina, and a man she was with left the bar together about 11:30 to 11:45. Tina and her friend rode in his truck. Me and Patty and Joni left in her truck. We all drove to Joni's house on Devon Street [one street north of Stacey's apartment]. *We were all drunk when we got to Joni's, but we decided to get some more beer. Me and the guy with my sister went to the Red Apple store and brought two six packs of long-necked Budweisers and Marlboro and Kool cigarettes to the counter. The clerk carded me, and I didn't have my license, so they wouldn't sell to me. I cursed the clerks. But my sister's friend showed them his license and bought the beer. We went back to Joni's.*

The five us drank some beer, and around 1 a.m., my sister left with that guy. Me and Patty spent the night at Joni's, sleeping on the couch. I got up about 7 a.m. I asked Patty if she wanted to go to the [Duchess of Dare] *Diner to get some breakfast. She said she didn't, so I walked there by myself.*

I stopped by Stacey's apartment. I got there sometime after 7 a.m. and picked up her newspaper at the bottom of the steps. I carried the newspaper to the top of the steps, where I found the outer door locked. I put the paper down and walked back down the steps. I knew I could have unlocked the door by just putting my hand through [a hole in] *the door and opening it, but I thought Stacey might have someone with her, so I left….I walked to the diner and ate breakfast.*

I called Joni's apartment to wake her up because she [had an errand to run]. *It was about 8 a.m. when I called her.*

He said he walked back to Joni's apartment, finding her and Patty there. He was with those two for most of the morning, he said, and also helped his brother move into a house on the island.

Later this afternoon, I went to the Green Dolphin. Sometime this afternoon, one of the bar workers told me about Stacey being found dead. I cried.

Brandon told the investigators that, besides last night, the last time he had seen Stacey was about five days earlier. He thought that was Tuesday, at her apartment. Clearly in response to questioning anticipating potential fingerprints, he said he was in her kitchen, her living room, her bedroom and her bathroom.

I did have sex with Stacey at that time. It was normal for her to have a mattress on the living room floor. She slept on the mattress most of the time.

I've got a record and have pulled time in prison. I was convicted of breaking and entering seven or eight years ago....

I do feel guilty about leaving Stacey, and if I had not left her, she would still be alive. We argued, but I never hit her. I could not have asked for a better person than Stacey....

I am short-tempered when I am drinking. I haven't smoked crack in about two months. I moved out of Stacey's apartment about a month ago, around Christmas. Stacey went home [to New Jersey] *for Christmas and tried to get me to go with her. I stayed here and started seeing Patty. I moved out of Stacey's apartment after she got home. I had thought about going back to Stacey, but Patty was pregnant with my child.*

My sister Tina, who found Stacey's body, told me Stacey's nipples had been cut off and she had been cut up. [Her nipples were not cut off, but that was one story going through the island rumor mill.]

Cliff told me on Friday night that Stacey had said something about killing herself. Cliff had tried to pick up Joni Newman last night at the Dolphin.

The door to Stacey's apartment was never locked. When I found it locked this morning, I felt that she had someone with her and did not try to go in.

Now I remember leaving the bar once by myself last night. I walked a couple of blocks before I returned.

In an apparent response to questioning, he said he did not remember seeing anyone on his walk.

I didn't go to Stacey's. The only reason I left was because Patty and me argued....I got back to the bar and later left with Patty and Joni.

I think Cliff had been smoking crack last night. I could tell it by looking at his eyes. I'd never seen him like he was last night, wanting money. In my opinion, Cliff may have killed Stacey.
I didn't cut or hurt Stacey. I'll be willing to take a polygraph any time.

Brandon gave a red-handled pocketknife of his to Chief Day. The investigators wrote that the interview ended at approximately 11:28 p.m.

One big question: How had Brandon not known about the killing until he got to the Green Dolphin Saturday afternoon? His sister found the body shortly after 2:00 p.m. Surely, she would have told him within minutes. And at the bar, he was just a few blocks over from Stacey's apartment, which was an obvious crime scene from shortly after 2:00 p.m. Saturday afternoon until late that night, with the mobile crime lab in the parking lot and numerous cars parked on the normally quiet street in front of the apartment building.

And why had Brandon gone by Stacey's apartment that Saturday morning?

Brandon's record, included breaking and entering, stretched back to his teenage years. One friend who loved Brandon in all his complexities told the author that he came by his criminality naturally from a rough childhood in Tarboro. He was an interesting cat, she said, often rising early to eat a big breakfast no matter how hungover he was from the night before or how little sleep he'd had. That friend said that, after Stacey was killed, Brandon told her, "Every time I close my eyes, I see her."

—∞—

ALSO ON SATURDAY, LIEUTENANT Colonel Williams of the sheriff's office and SBI agent Eric Hooks interviewed Patty Rowe. She was a knockout admired by many local men, around the same height and weight as Stacey, with Rowe standing about five feet, four inches tall and 110 pounds. Rowe had grown up on the Outer Banks. She said at one point that she met Brandon the previous fall in the Green Dolphin and, at another point, that she met him through her brother, Ray Griggs, when he had rented the apartment beside Stacey's when Mike was living with her.

Rowe was tough, easily holding her own, even with a bit of wit with the investigators.

She said she had been drinking in the Dolphin the night before, after she got off work there, and saw Stacey, according to the investigators' notes handwritten notes in cursive. Rowe said that Stacey was "kinda popular" and "everybody liked her, she was very polite."

Rowe said she was "kinda upset" that night because she was arguing with Brandon.

> *What were you arguing about? the investigators asked.*
> *Rowe: I woke up grouchy.*
> *Investigators: Is Mike Brandon your boyfriend?*
> *Rowe: Yes.*
> *Investigators: How often do you and Mike argue?*
> *Rowe: This is probably the second time. We've been dating since early December. Nurse told me I was pregnant.*
> *Investigators: Is Mike the father?*
> *Rowe: Yes.*
> *Investigators: Marriage plans?*
> *Rowe: We haven't talked about it.*

She confirmed Brandon's story of going to Joni Newman's Manteo house, one street over from Stacey's apartment, with him and friends late Friday night. But although Brandon said he had left the apartment alone early Saturday morning and walked up to Stacey's apartment and then to the Duchess of Dare restaurant, Rowe said he did not leave Newman's home until 9:15 a.m. on Saturday, when he left with her.

She said she found out about Stacey at work at the Green Dolphin that Saturday. One of the bartenders, crying, told her that Stacey had been killed.

> *Investigators: Any idea who would do this to Stacey?*
> *Rowe: No.*
> *Investigators: Did she have any enemies?*
> *Rowe: No. I don't think she liked me. Got in a fight one time, but don't remember when, after Christmas. No cross words after that, mutual. Physical fight…She (Stacey) found out about me and Mike.*
> *Investigators: How did the fight end?*
> *Rowe: …I hit her and tried to kick her; she pulled my hair. We were both drinking. Mike tried to break us up.*

(In a phone call with her father shortly before her slaying, Stacey had talked about the fight with Patty, saying, "It was the lowest point in my life." Ed Stanton Jr. said his father begged Stacey to come home to Jersey.)

Rowe said she had been in Stacey's apartment once with Brandon and another couple, when Stacey was in Jersey with her parents over Christmas.

Investigators: Do you have a temper?

Rowe: Sometimes, not really that bad.

Investigators: Does Mike have a temper?

Rowe: Really a nice guy, sweet, would never do that. I was with him [Friday night].

Investigators: Is Mike capable of hurting Stacey?

Rowe: Not at all.

Investigators: Would you consider your relationship with Mike strained?

Rowe: Yes.

Investigators: You and Stacey weren't the best of friends, were you?

Rowe: No.

Investigators: Did you have any conversation with Stacey when she came in the Green Dolphin?

Rowe: Just [to] *ask her if she wanted a wine cooler and that's all.*

Investigators: Does Mike want you to have a baby?

Rowe: Yes.

Investigators: Did he ever mention abortion to you?

Rowe: Yes, then said he was sorry. Last night we really weren't getting along.

Investigators: Do you think Mike [was] *still in love with Stacey?*

Rowe: No, just had feelings for her. Told me he was going to leave [his] *clothes and not bother with them.*

Investigators: During Christmas you went to Stacey's [apartment] *to see Mike, didn't you?*

Rowe: Yes, we were seeing each other while they were dating.

Investigators: Do you have a knife?

Rowe: Yes, only in my kitchen.

Investigators: Christmas the last time you were at Stacey's?

Rowe: Uh huh, only time there.

Investigators: When did Mike go to Stacey's last if you know?

Rowe: Mike went and got his stuff New Year's Day. He went back one other time. Came to my house January 2 or January 3. He and I went together every night at the Green Dolphin.

Friday night, Rowe said, she had a wine cooler, a half a beer and, when she went walking near the bar by herself, a small joint. She had a small buzz, she said. The bar owner, Ginger Tramontano, would not let her have more to drink because she was pregnant, she said.

She said that when Mike left the bar briefly that night, he told her he walked around the block.

The next morning, she said, Mike had breakfast with her at Joni's house. (He had told investigators he ate at the Duchess of Dare.)

The interview ended shortly thereafter.

—∽—

AT 4:45 SUNDAY MORNING, SBI agent Honeycutt cleared the crime scene. Stacey's body was soon loaded into a hearse to be transported for autopsy to Pitt Memorial Hospital in Greenville, North Carolina, a drive of about two hours. The woman who had loved the company of her island friends was gone and alone.

Honeycutt made no note of the fact that the crime scene had been compromised by the failure of Manteo police and the Dare County Sheriff's Office to secure it, allowing the numerous bystanders to walk through. In her *CounterClock* podcast in 2020 on the case, Manteo native Delia D'Ambra noted the crime scene contamination.

Locals who had trampled the scene knew that it had been compromised, and they told friends who told their friends. Word also quickly spread that Stacey's breast and vagina had been slashed.

5

HUNTING THE MURDER WEAPON

The pathologist told us that the blade from a box-cutter knife "would be consistent with how she was cut.... The cuts on her were generally not over a half-inch deep and she was cut with a sharp instrument."
—SBI agent Kent Inscoe, in a court hearing

Islanders of long memory knew there was a grim sense of déjà vu to the crime. They knew the nights when whitetail deer dance in the marshes and evil hangs heavy as clouds. One night twenty-three years before, in July 1967, another beautiful girl, Brenda Joyce Holland, had been killed on the island. She had rented a room on the same street as Stacey's, just a few hundred yards away. Brenda was the nineteen-year-old makeup supervisor for *The Lost Colony*. She went missing, and her bloated body was found floating in the Sound after a massive five-day search. Pathologists found she had been strangled and, quite possibly, raped.

Stacey and the rest of the characters you'll meet in this book were children when Brenda was killed. Their generation grew up hearing their parents talk about Brenda's case as they spread out large broadsheets of the local newspaper, the *Coastland Times*, on kitchen tables and read the latest stories about Brenda's case, often accompanied by the pageant PR shot of Brenda, her blonde hair cut in a bob, a string of pearls around her graceful neck— the same neck that the autopsy said a killer had put some type of cord around. Children shivered as they heard their parents gossip.

The case had become legend for their generation, evil that law enforcement failed to solve. That had been in the supposed "Summer of Love" and had marked the end of innocence for many in the generation of Stacey's parents, the point, looking back, when they realized that the barren sands they loved would surrender to McMansions and problems from "the real world" they once escaped in a five-minute, open-windowed, sea-sprayed ride across a bridge from the mainland were no longer escapable.

For Stacey's generation, the hedonistic, hard-drinking, nonjudgmental lifestyle still reigned, but some locals began to couple their drinking with cocaine, with bar bathrooms being places to share "key hits," a bit of coke on the end of a key to be snorted, and later, back at cottages, framed seaside portraits from absent parents taken down from the walls and placed on tables where long lines of white powder were snorted through straws and rolled-up dollar bills. The TV series *Miami Vice*, with its rock 'n' roll MTV style depicting undercover agents chasing coke dealers, had just ended in 1989, and many locals had loved it, sniffing coke lines as they watched. Some locals smoked crack cocaine, a more intense high that, for the busted, especially if they were Black, usually resulted in stiffer punishment.

Stacey's story would become as legendary as Brenda's. It was another mystery on the island, mysteries that had begun with that of the Lost Colony.

Brenda, just like Stacey, was a newcomer to the island who had ingratiated herself to the locals. A man who had dated Stacey about a year before she was slain later told the author, between tears, "She was a good girl. She was too friendly, and that was probably her demise."

The Dare County Sheriff's Office, the SBI and the Manteo Police Department never solved Brenda's case. Their numerous mistakes have been well-documented.

The killing of Brenda and that of Stacey bookended an era of easy-to-solve murder cases for law enforcement. The slayings in between, and before Brenda, for that matter, had, for the most part, been simple to solve, cuttings and shootings.

Now, in 1990, the investigators were faced with their first challenging case since 1967. In 1990, as in 1967, the locals were spooked on their normally peaceful island, knowing that the killer was among them. Twenty-three years later, the pressure was just as heavy to catch Stacey's killer. And, after the Holland case, the doubts were heavy among locals that the investigators could protect them and get the killer.

It wasn't like the islanders didn't know violence. It was the salt air they breathed from birth, bloody fistfights with noses broken and teeth flying, fishing mishaps out at sea, hooks buried into flesh, fingers caught in lines and maimed, lightning searing flesh, mountainous waves knocking rusty trawlers asunder. But who-done-it murders were a rarity.

Stacey was one of their own, one of the few wash-ins whom they accepted and came to love. Manteo is protective and loving to those they accept. Stacey lived just a few blocks over from the home of her beloved family friend, Boyd Midgett. If she wasn't safe, who was? There was considerable fear on the island, especially among women. Gail Hutchison, a *Lost Colony* alumnus spending her first winter on the island, slept with a butcher's knife wedged in the slat board under her bed.

And there was another consideration with Stacey's case: The island was in the midst of its revitalization, and spring and summer, with their crucial tourist dollars, were coming fast. The killer had to be caught, and quickly.

—⁂—

SUNDAY MORNING, FEBRUARY 4, the morgue at Pitt Memorial Hospital, Greensville, North Carolina. At 8:00 a.m., pathologist L.S. "Stan" Harris performed the autopsy on Stacey's body. Harris wrote:

> *The body is that of a well-developed, slender young adult white woman appearing the given age of 28 years or slightly younger....When first examined at this facility, the only type of clothing on the body is a jersey blouse/shirt slightly pulled up at the waist. Blood is heavily soaked about the neck of this garment....*
>
> *Items of jewelry on the body include a gold metal necklace and a gold metal bracelet on the left wrist....Scalp hair is basically medium brown with long segments of blond highlights; the hair length is midway between short and shoulder length. The facial features are partially obscured by smeared blood over the lower portions....*
>
> *The anterior aspect of the neck displays a large number of sharply incised wounds, two of which are longer than the others and extend more deeply than the others....*[SBI Agent Honeycutt would later testify there were fourteen "superficial type wounds" in addition to the two deep wounds.]
>
> *There is an obliquely inclined wound over the right breast four inches in length....Two separate nearly parallel incised wounds appear in a vertical*

long axis…extending to the vulva and through the crus of the vulva just to
the right of the clitoris.…These vertical incisions measure 2.0 and 2.25
inches in length and have been produced by cuts from below upward.

Harris summed up his report:

FINAL DIAGNOSIS
Multiple incised wounds of anterior neck
Transection of left common carotid artery and left jugular vein and of
upper larynx.
Interior and external loss of blood.
Multiple additional incised wounds of posterior neck, right breast and
vagina, largely inflicted during or immediately after death.

OPINION
Cause of Death: Incised wounds of anterior neck with transection of
major blood vessels and consequent loss of blood.
Manner of Death: Homicide.
Comment: The infliction of the sharply incised wounds to the breast
and vaginal region while the deceased was dying or already dead
suggests a fetishistic activity on the part of the assailant.

There was no evidence of rape.

—⁂—

ALTHOUGH THE WRITTEN AUTOPSY report would take some time, Dr. Harris
phoned the investigators with a brief summary. The strong suggestion of
"fetishistic activity" would have been of particular interest. The killer held a
terrible anger for Stacey that seemed intensely personal.

The hours since her body had been found were ticking away fast. Time
is the enemy in the early phases of a homicide probe. The memories of
witnesses, often diminished by alcohol and drugs, are fast fading, and
evidence can be as well. And most important, killers can flee. In that early
phase, investigators often work around the clock, going without sleep for as
many as three days.

At 9:10 a.m. on Sunday at the Dare County Sheriff's Office in Manteo,
SBI agent Eric Hooks and Manteo police chief Day interviewed Richard
Scarborough. He was dating Mike Brandon's sister, Tina, although he

was not the man with her late Friday night into early Saturday morning. Scarborough said he'd been at the Green Dolphin Friday night:

> *Stacey still cared for Mike. She told me she had sex with him last Tuesday. As far as I know, she wasn't dating anybody else.*

—⁂—

Sunday morning at 10:55 at the sheriff's office, SBI agents David Wooten and Inscoe and Chief Day took another run at Mike Brandon. In response to questioning, Brandon said:

> *I have never cut anyone with a knife. I do carry one, and have threatened to cut people, but I've never actually cut anyone....I threatened a guy once with a knife, but I did not cut him. I've never carried a box* [cutter] *knife. The only knife I carried was the red-handled pocketknife that Chief Day took from me.*
>
> *I'm still willing to take a polygraph. I'll cooperate in any way that I can.*

The interview ended about 11:25 that Sunday morning.

—⁂—

At about 11:15 that Sunday morning at the sheriff's office, SBI agent Hooks interviewed thirty-year-old Rick Willis of Manteo, a friend of Stacey's who had been in the Green Dolphin Friday night:

> *I'd known Stacey since December 1988. I saw her about two or three times a week. Stacey was a trusting person who didn't lock her car door or her house door. She confided in me about her relationships with Mike and Cliff. She told me that she was still in love with Mike and did not know how to handle the fact that Mike was the father of Patty's unborn baby. Stacey told me that Mike and Cliff smoked crack together and that is how they became friends.*
>
> *Stacey and Cliff were not friends. Spencer would often come around her apartment early in the day to get a drink and hang around. She told me that she'd have to ease Spencer out of the apartment. She told me she felt uneasy about Spencer coming over to her apartment, but she allowed him entrance because she did not want to be rude.*

Recently, on January 28, 1990, I'd replaced some sheet rock in Stacey's apartment. I used a utility knife Stacey had at the apartment. Stacey told me she'd found the knife at work. I left the knife and blades at her apartment.

Agent Inscoe would later say that he and the other investigators told the pathologist, Dr. Harris, about the box cutter missing from the apartment. Harris told them that the blade from that knife "would be consistent with how she was cut.…The cuts on her were generally not over a half-inch deep and she was cut with a sharp instrument," Inscoe said.

Investigators began searching for the murder weapon.

—m—

AT ABOUT 11:50 A.M. in the sheriff's office that Sunday, Agent Hooks and David Wooten interviewed Marty Madden, who lived in the apartment beside Stacey's, where Patty Rowe's brother Ray Griggs had lived until a few months earlier. Madden told them:

I got home from work about 10:50 p.m. Saturday. About 11:15 p.m., I went up to Todd Daniels' apartment and talked to him and his girlfriend until 12 or 12:30 a.m., then went back to my apartment.…Around 1 to 1:15 a.m., I heard Stacey's voice through the wall of my apartment. I recognized her voice because it was very distinctive. Also, around 1 to 1:15 am., I heard someone walking up the steps to the apartment. I can't remember exactly if I heard the steps before I heard the voice or after I heard Stanton's voice. I took some cough syrup before going to bed and went to sleep. I believe I slept soundly because of the cough syrup and did not hear anything the rest of the night.

"The interview concluded at approximately 2:15 p.m.," Hooks wrote. The investigators kept up their search for that elusive murder weapon.

6

CALLING STACEY'S NAME

I could also see a lot of blood.
—Tina Bass in an interview with the SBI

Sunday morning, the day after Stacey's body was found, SBI agents Kent Inscoe and David Wooten interviewed Mike Brandon's sister, Tina Bass, at the sheriff's office. Bass told them she worked at the Duchess of Dare until about 9:30 p.m. the previous Friday, then walked over to the Green Dolphin:

I met my brother Mike and Joni Newman and shot pool.
Cliff Spencer was there.....Mike was talking to Cliff, and I heard Cliff
say that he was leaving, there were too many white people there. He did
leave after talking to Mike, that must have been around 10.

She said her brother left the bar once but was gone only about five minutes. "We stayed at the bar until 11, 11:30, maybe even 12 midnight," she said.

She confirmed her brother's story: that she, a male friend, Joni Newman, Patty and Mike left the bar and went to Joni's apartment, and Mike and her male friend had gone to a convenience store for beer and cigarettes. They were gone about ten minutes, she said. She and her male friend left Joni's apartment about 12:30 a.m., she said, and drove to her home, where they spent the night. She went to work at the diner at about 6:45 a.m. the next day, she said. At about 2:05 p.m., she said, Terri Williams, the Dare County deputy who also worked at the restaurant, told her to go check on Stacey, who was supposed to be at work by 2:00 p.m. Bass said she drove the short distance to Stacey's apartment, seeing Stacey's car parked out front.

I got out of my car and walked up the steps to her apartment. There was a newspaper at the top of the steps that I picked up. The [storm] *door was locked, so I reached* [through the hole in the door] *and unlocked it....I entered and laid the newspaper on a chair in the living room. I walked down the hall to the bedroom, calling Stacey's name....The only light was from the aquarium.*

Then she saw Stacey.

I could also see a lot of blood. I called for Stacey, but she did not answer. I panicked and went back to the diner where I told what I had seen. I told Terri Williams they needed to get the deputies, Stacey was hurt and there was blood everywhere.

Terri called Central Radio and gave them Stacey's location. I went back to Stacey's with Terri. We both walked into Stacey's apartment, where Terri turned on the light in the living room. Terri looked at me and said, "Let's get out of here, she's dead." Me and Terri went outside, and a Manteo police officer soon arrived, then, the EMTs....

I never heard Stacey say she was scared of anyone. She had been depressed recently, probably because of her breakup with Mike. Stacey was mad with Patty, Mike's new girlfriend....

Stacey had told me Mike came to see her in her apartment Thursday, and they "went to bed." Mike must have been there before 10:30 a.m., because Stacey came to work [at the Duchess of Dare] *at 10:30.*

Friday at the diner, Stacey kept telling me to talk to Mike, that she wanted him back.

The interview ended at about 12:05 p.m. It left big questions that the investigators did not ask in the interview summary they filed. How had Bass not seen Stacey's body in the living room, even with dim light, walking right past her to the bedroom before she turned around and finally saw the body in the living room? The day was overcast, but it's likely some hazy sunlight would still have been coming through the windows of the second-floor apartment. And how could she, especially as a woman, have not smelled the overpowering odor of blood as soon as she walked in?

The day after Stacey was killed, a deputy picked up Cliff Spencer for questioning by this road in his hometown of Columbia, North Carolina. *John Railey.*

Also, she said she and Terri Williams reentered the apartment together. Terri Williams had told investigators that she had Bass wait outside when they returned to the apartment, and she went in alone. And contrary to what Bass said, Williams said she did not cut on the light, not wanting to disturb the crime scene.

In her *CounterClock* podcast, Delia D'Ambra also noted Bass's contradiction of Williams's statement.

Finally, other witnesses told the investigators that Stacey and Mike got together Tuesday of that week, not Thursday.

—⁓—

ALSO THAT SUNDAY, CATHY Rogers of the Green Dolphin came back by the sheriff's office and talked to Lieutenant Colonel Williams. At about two o'clock on Saturday morning, she said, she and a friend had gone by Joni Newman's house to give Patty Rowe a ride home. Nobody answered the door, she said. Investigators did not note in the summary why Rogers was coming to get Rowe. Rogers said in June 2023 that she did not remember going by Newman's house that night.

While continuing to consider Brandon as a suspect, the investigators ran Clifton Spencer's record, learning that he had an outstanding cocaine charge from New Jersey and that he was from Columbia, North Carolina, about a forty-five-minute drive west of Manteo on Highway 64. The tiny town is the seat of the rural county of Tyrrell. That Sunday, the investigators coordinated with the Tyrrell Sheriff's Office, arranging to have Spencer picked up for questioning and brought to that office. Tyrrell deputy Steve Bell found Spencer on Railroad Street in Columbia, a rundown neighborhood with a wooded, swampy stretch where druggies hung out. Bell, who knew Spencer, stopped his cruiser and asked Spencer to come to his office and talk to some Dare County investigators. Bell did not go into detail. Spencer got in the car.

Spencer, thirty-two, was essentially homeless, working odd jobs and living between the homes of friends and relatives, wherever he could find a bed. Sometimes, he crashed on the front porch of his grandmother's house. She'd been dead since 1977, but the family had kept the house. Spencer was a "toothbrush in his pocket" kind of guy.

The Tyrrell County lawmen placed Spencer, alone, in a small office in their sheriff's department to await the Dare County lawmen.

Above: The Tyrrell County Sheriff's Office and jail in Columbia, where Cliff Spencer was first held. *John Railey*.

Opposite: Through this window in the Tyrrell sheriff's office can be seen the small room where Cliff Spencer awaited questioning in Stacey's slaying. *John Railey.*

The lawmen left crime scene photos of Stacey's body on a desk. The photos were turned upside down, toward the holder of the desk, but they clearly showed Stacey had been stabbed. The photos were obviously left there for Spencer to "accidentally" see, an old law-enforcement trick to scare defendants into a confession.

The initial investigative team was falling into place: SBI agent Kent Inscoe, Dare County colonel Jasper Williams, and Manteo police chief Steve Day. Day would later say his department had jurisdiction in the case. He was right, but the sheriff's office shared jurisdiction in Manteo. The SBI entered the case at Day's request. The case file does not indicate who led the probe. SBI supervisor Bill Godley played a limited role. Dare County sheriff Bert Austin was a good lawman but gave his top officers, including Jasper Williams, wide sway.

SBI agent Tony Cummings helped out in the early weeks of the case, as did other agents to a lesser degree. Inscoe and Cummings had long experience with murder cases. Inscoe, who had been with the SBI since 1972, would later testify that by the time the probe of Stacey's slaying began, he had been the case agent on "probably over fifty" murder cases and "probably assisted on over a hundred more." Williams, who had been in law enforcement since 1974, was a veteran deputy, but Dare County saw few murder cases, especially challenging ones like Stacey's.

There was turmoil in the department before Chief Day's hiring, as Mayor Mollie Fearing noted in a meeting of the town commissioners as Day was hired:

> *Mayor Fearing stated that the Police Department needs a chief immediately because once again one of the officers has taken confidential information from the police office file and given that information to the person being investigated. She added that this wouldn't have happened if the Department had a qualified chief on staff.*

Day was paid $25,000 a year, equivalent to about $59,000 in 2024 dollars, a decent salary for a small-town police chief in a normally quiet town. His job had not been that hard. For example, in October 1989, he reported to the town board of commissioners that, in September, his department "responded to 79 calls and complaints resulting in 7 arrests, 4 traffic arrests, 15 town citations issued, and investigated 4 motor vehicle accidents."

Day, however, clashed with the town board. He resigned in January 1990, and the board accepted his resignation, with an effective date of January 30. But just days later, on February 2, 1990, the day before Stacey was killed, Day had apparently worked out his problems with the board. The board, including Commissioner Boyd Midgett, voted unanimously "to accept Chief Day's letter of reinstatement."

7

Spencer Denies Killing Stacey

*I didn't have anything to do with Stacey's death and will be willing
to take a polygraph.*
—*Clifton Eugene Spencer to investigators*

O n Sunday afternoon, February 4, at 1:25, Agent Inscoe and Chief
Day met with Cliff Spencer in a small room in the old brick
building on a side street near Columbia's small downtown that
houses the Tyrrell sheriff's office and jail.

Tyrrell, a county with wide expanses of fields and woods by the
Scuppernong River and the Albemarle Sound, is home to bobcats, bald
eagles, peregrine falcons, alligators and endangered red wolves. It's wild and
wonderful country but, for myriad Outer Banks visitors, just a stop on the
way to the beach. Spencer and many of his friends saw it the same way. They
loved to ride the two-lane 64 to Outer Banks, where the real "wildlife" was.

That Friday night, Spencer had caught a ride to the Banks after an
afternoon of beer drinking and doing cocaine with friends. He had a lot
of Manteo friends, having driven a truck for Kellogg Supply and Griggs
Lumber. He had lived in Manteo in the past few years.

Cliff had been reasonably flush that Friday night, with thirty dollars from
chopping wood with some relatives and cleaning a laundromat, not "broke"
as Brandon said he had been.

During the interview, Spencer sat on one side of a table. The two
white investigators sat on the other side. The investigators told him that

Stacey had been killed and they wanted to talk to him about it. The investigators wrote that they read Spencer his rights and he agreed to talk. They said Spencer never asked them if Stacey had been killed by a gun or knife, despite their leading questions on that subject. Spencer denied killing Stacey.

Spencer would later dispute much of what the investigators quoted him on from that interview and in several subsequent interviews. He never signed any of the statements the investigators attributed to him, and he never wrote his own statement. The interviews were not audiotaped or videotaped. That was not required in North Carolina at the time, although the recording equipment was available, and some law enforcement agencies used it. The investigators' notes on their interviews with Spencer and others are summaries of the interviews that often lack the give-and-take, question-and-answer form of such interviews, although many investigators in North Carolina had long been providing that detailed form. Most of the reports in Spencer's case are typewritten, but several are handwritten, often written weeks after the interviews occurred.

The investigators said Spencer told them on that Sunday:

> *I knew Stacey. She was a friend of mine. I was in her apartment Friday night. I didn't know she was dead. No one told me she was dead or had been killed until Agent Inscoe just told me. When I got here to the sheriff's office, I did hear the dispatcher say something about a murder suspect being in custody, but I didn't know who she was talking about....*
>
> *Friday night at the Green Dolphin, I talked to my friend Mike Brandon. I saw Stacey and waved to her, but we didn't talk. I drank several beers. Mike was shooting pool, and Stacey had been standing in the corner when I got there. Mike's new girlfriend, Patty, was seated at the bar.*
>
> *While I was at the bar, Stacey got upset. Stacey was drunk, and Mike wanted her to go home. She and Mike had words and Stacey left. About 15 minutes after Stacey left, I told Mike I would be back and left. I don't wear a watch but think that was between 8 and 9. I started walking and ended up in Stacey's parking lot....I saw her standing on her apartment steps, talking to a white guy in the parking lot I did not know. She asked me:*
>
> *"Cliff, is that you?"*
>
> *"Yes."*
>
> *"What the hell did I do?"* [referring to her words with Mike in the bar]

Spencer said he walked up the stairs and entered Stacey's apartment with her. The white man in the parking lot left. Spencer continued, according to the SBI:

I fixed myself a vodka drink and talked with Stacey about Mike. Stacey was crying. She had been drinking, but she was talking OK and seemed like she knew what she was doing. She wanted me to go back to the bar and talk to Mike, to talk him into coming back to the apartment to talk with her. I stayed at Stacey's for about 45 minutes before going back to the bar to talk to Mike for Stacey.

Back at the bar, I asked Mike to go to Stacey's and talk to her. He told me he was grown and would do what he wanted to do. I drank three to four beers while I watched people play pool....

About a week earlier, Stacey had told me that Mike was coming back to her. She was happy.

While I was at the bar the second time, I was confronted by a white man about 50 cents the man allegedly left on a pool table. I had picked up the 50 cents, but the money was mine [so he could challenge the winner of the next game]. *The confrontation blew over, and I kept my 50 cents.*

Mike was still at the bar....I told Mike I had a friend with some drugs and asked him if he wanted to do any. He said no....I asked Mike for some money to buy drugs, but he would not give me any....I left the bar by myself around 11. Mike was still there....

I walked back to Stacey's. A white guy was sitting there talking to her. I didn't know his name but knew of him. He was drunk. He'd been in the bar before Mike and Stacey had their argument.

I sat down and had a drink with the guy....While we were talking, Stacey, who'd been wearing the short skirt at the bar, got up and up left the living room, but returned a short time later wearing gray sweatpants and the same top she'd had on earlier. After we talked for a while, around midnight, this guy said he was going back to the bar. He asked me to go, but he left by himself. The TV was on, and I think MTV [Music Television] *was on....*

Stacey asked me what Mike had said, and I told her [about Mike refusing to come see her]. *She cried.*

According to the investigators, Spencer said he smoked some crack cocaine alone at Stacey's apartment, and, when his crack was done, Stacey gave him thirty-five dollars to go out and buy her some crack. He walked

After lawmen finished their initial round of questioning, they led Cliff Spencer up this narrow stairway in the Columbia sheriff's office to a cell where he was held on an outstanding drug charge from New Jersey. *John Railey.*

around Manteo looking for a buy, he said, but was unsuccessful and returned to Stacey's apartment about 12:30 or 1:00 a.m., finding the door locked and all the lights off.

He walked to a friend's Manteo mobile home, waited for him to get home and walked around for a while before his friend, Wayne Morris, returned home around 4:30 a.m., Spencer said. He went to sleep at his friend's home, he said. The next morning, he said, he caught a ride back to Columbia.

He told the investigators that he had spent the night at Stacey's several times. Brandon was always there when he did, he said, except for one time. He had never had sexual intercourse with Stacey, he said, but had engaged in oral sex with her two to three times. (Spencer would later deny ever having said any of that.)

Friday night, Spencer said, Stacey had sat on his lap, and they kissed. His fingerprints would be all over the apartment, he said. He told them about his New Jersey cocaine charge, of which the investigators were already aware. Spencer added:

> I didn't have anything to do with Stacey's death and will be willing to take a polygraph.

The interview ended at about 3:20 p.m., almost two hours after it started.

Back in Manteo at 5:20 p.m. at the sheriff's office, Agent Inscoe and Chief Day interviewed Wayne Morris, whose trailer Spencer said he had crashed at early Saturday. Morris confirmed Spencer had been there, arriving between 4:00 and 5:00 a.m., waiting for him. Spencer appeared to be high on crack, Morris said. Morris said he left for work about 6:30 a.m. Saturday, and Spencer was still there, asleep. Morris said there was no blood on Spencer's clothes when he came in that morning. Later SBI testing found no blood in the trailer. Morris told the author in July 2023 that he remembered the events well because it was his birthday weekend and that Spencer did not kill Stacey.

The investigators contacted New Jersey authorities and arranged to have Spencer held in the Columbia jail on the Jersey cocaine charge. A Tyrrell deputy led Spencer up a small metal staircase to one of the few cells on the second floor of the building and locked him up. Spencer's father, Harry, soon visited him in the jail. The father didn't waste time: "Son, did you kill that girl? You can tell me. You don't have to lie to me, I'm your father."

Spencer told his father he did not kill her. "Stacey was my friend," he said.

8

BRANDON ATTENDS STACEY'S FUNERAL

Mike did it.
—Stacey Stanton's mother, Maryanne, after her daughter's funeral

At the sheriff's office in Manteo at 6:20 Sunday night, SBI agents Eric Hooks and David Wooten interviewed Richard "Dick" Fugate of Manteo, who'd been at Stacey's apartment Friday night. He was, apparently, the white man Cliff had seen there. Fugate, who sometimes played guitar at the Green Dolphin, said he had seen Stacey earlier that night at the Green Dolphin:

> *I'd known Stacey for a couple of years. We were friends, but not close ones. She told me about Mike Brandon, and I talked to her about problems with Mike Brandon, and I told her about my relationship with my girlfriend. Stacey left the bar between 8:30 and 9. I stayed at the bar and drank until I was mildly buzzed.*
>
> *At about 9:30 p.m., I left the bar to walk around. I walked over to Stacey's apartment, getting there about 9:40 p.m....Stacey was alone. I had a mixed drink. Stacey asked me to go back to the bar and convince Brandon to come over. I declined.*
>
> *A tall Black man came to the apartment. He introduced himself as a guy from Tarboro. I'm from Tarboro, recognized the name he gave and knew he was not that guy, that he was using a false name. The Black guy at Stacey's had short hair and a small mustache.*

> *The Black man accused me of not liking Black people. I got uncomfortable and left about five minutes after this guy got to Stacey's. I felt uneasy about leaving her in the apartment with him. I went back to the Green Dolphin. My girlfriend called me there about 10:30, offering to come get me and give me a ride home. I declined. I stayed at the pub until closing and caught a ride home with a bartender.*

The interview ended at 6:55 p.m. Apparently, Fugate was the unnamed man Spencer said he had met at Stacey's apartment.

—⁂—

ON MONDAY, AT ABOUT 10:20 a.m., Lieutenant Colonel Williams, Chief Day and some of the SBI agents met at a Columbia restaurant to discuss reinterviewing Spencer and persuading him to take a polygraph. Deputy Steve Bell of the Tyrrell County Sheriff's Office "entered the restaurant and stated that he had spoken briefly with Spencer on that morning and that Spencer had stated to him, 'Man, I didn't kill that girl. I don't have any blood on my clothes,'" according to notes taken by Chief Day.

Later that Monday morning at the Columbia jail, Day wrote in handwritten notes, that, with Spencer and Columbia attorney Charles Ogletree present, Spencer said that he and Stacey were engaged in foreplay, but Spencer "was unable to achieve an erection."

"He got up, went to the bath and washed up, dressed and left the apartment," Day wrote.

Spencer said in May 2023 that he never told the investigators that and it was not true. They asked him leading questions in that regard, he said, but he never confirmed their allegations. Ogletree was not his attorney of record for Stacey's case, Spencer said. He had been counsel to his family on previous matters, Spencer said, and was helping out in the initial stages of the murder case, although he was his attorney on the New Jersey drug charge. Spencer said Ogletree often told him to stop talking to the investigators, but Spencer said he was just trying to help find the killer. Spencer said that Day seemed the most sympathetic of the investigators, often seeming to doubt, albeit silently, his fellow investigators' emphasis on him. Day's notes on that Monday interview:

Day: I asked Spencer if he cut Stacey. He looked away and gave no response. I asked Spencer if Stacey was alive when he left the apartment. He responded, "Chief, if I had killed Stacey, I would tell you!"

Spencer then stated that he was through talking and was not going to answer any more questions. Atty [sic] Ogletree agreed.

—◊◊◊—

THE INVESTIGATORS PERSUADED SPENCER to take a polygraph test later that Monday at the Tyrrell County jail. Before Spencer took the test, Chief Day said in a handwritten note, "I noticed that Spencer appeared to be very nervous and was attempting to clean his fingernails on a white piece of paper that appeared to be a napkin. This napkin was removed from a trashcan and submitted to the SBI for trace evidence." (None was found.)

SBI agent W.H. "Bill" Thompson conducted the polygraph test, asking Spencer three questions:

"Did you cut Stacey?"

"Did you cut Stacey in the apartment?"

"Were you there when Stacey was cut?"

Spencer replied "No" to each question. When the test was done, Thompson told him he failed it, that the results showed deception on his part. Spencer was incredulous and told the investigators there must have been a mistake.

The same day, Agent Inscoe asked Spencer to give blood, hair and saliva samples and fingernail clippings and scrapings. Spencer refused. Inscoe called the district attorney's office and secured a search warrant for the items. Inscoe served the warrant and, that Monday night, drove Spencer from the Columbia jail to the hospital in Edenton, a drive of about forty-five minutes. A doctor there gathered the samples, including by cutting about fifty hairs from Spencer's head and about fifty hairs from his pubic region. Spencer was thoroughly humiliated.

—◊◊◊—

AT A PRESS CONFERENCE in Manteo Monday night, Captain Sam Ball of the Manteo Police Department said the investigation was continuing and that he could say nothing, but confirmed Stacey's death was caused from bleeding as a result of multiple cuts of her neck. When asked if he thought the police would solve the killing, he said, "I would like to say we will. I'm not sure."

Manteo police captain Sam Ball. *Drew C. Wilson via the Outer Banks History Center, State Archives.*

Questioned on whether the people of Manteo had anything to worry about, Ball said, "Personally I don't feel they do."

He did not reveal that a suspect was in custody. But lawmen were privately reaching out to island women, telling them that they should not be afraid, that the violence against Stacey was personal and they were safe.

Mike Brandon, Stacey's ex-boyfriend who had implicated Spencer, sat on a front row at the press conference, looking sad-faced and shaken, surrounded by his new girlfriend Patty Rowe and other friends from the Green Dolphin.

Captain Ball looked over at Brandon. He knew Brandon and thought of him as "a dirtball" capable of killing Stacey. He thought Brandon's shaken appearance was faked. But Ball kept his silence. He was not on the investigative team.

Two days later, Brandon was one of about twenty people from the island who journeyed to South Jersey for Stacey's funeral at the Northfield church in which she was raised, St. Bernadette's. The coffin was closed due to the slashing the killer had wrought on Stacey's neck. Monsignor Clarke led the service. About four hundred people packed the church, with many of them afterward joining the long line of cars driving a few miles to the cemetery where Clarke said a few words over Stacey's coffin, which was later lowered into the ground beside plots designated for her parents.

One of Stacey's friends, her cousin Meg Horton, was bothered by something she noticed at the funeral. Horton was seated by her mother, behind Brandon. She remembered that he was crying, a mess. But something wasn't right, she said. A friend from Manteo was seated beside him, she said, but that friend, apparently his sister, Tina, never reached out to him and there was a space between them. "She wasn't consoling him," said Horton.

The Stantons had never met Brandon until then, although Stacey may have confided to her father about him. Horton wasn't the only person who got a bad feeling about Brandon.

Manteo police captain Sam Ball at a press conference two days after Stacey's murder in February 1990. Suspect Mike Brandon, appearing shaken, is on the far right, having shown up as a spectator. *Drew C. Wilson via the Outer Banks History Center, State Archives.*

Stacey's gravestone in Northfield, New Jersey. *Sharon Stanton.*

BACK AT THE STANTON house, Horton said, Stacey's mother told her: "Mike did it."

Ed Stanton Jr. said of his mother: "She just said right from the start that she knew he did it."

In the days ahead, the family picked up Stacey's belongings from the apartment, those not entered into evidence. Ed Jr. lovingly took in Stacey's cat, Molly.

9

"Not a F—— Man in Here"

Mike was angry, glaring at the wall, hostile-like, mad at the world.
—*Barbara "Bobbi" McGuinness on Stacey's ex-boyfriend Mike Brandon in the Green Dolphin Pub, hours before Stacey was killed*

Late Tuesday afternoon, at 4:55 p.m., SBI agent Inscoe and Chief Day interviewed Barbara "Bobbi" McGuinness of Manteo at the sheriff's office. She had been friends with Stacey and ran a painting business and sometimes employed Brandon. She talked about tension in the Green Dolphin the previous Friday between Brandon and Stacey:

> *Joni Newman and I were walking in the Green Dolphin about 7 p.m. when we met Patty Rowe outside. She was very upset and told me, "I need to talk." Joni walked off with Patty [Mike's new girlfriend]. Once I got inside the pub, I saw Mike shooting pool. "What's going on with Patty?" I asked him.*
>
> *"Fuck Patty," he said.*
>
> *I walked to another part of the room, by the jukebox, where Stacey was. Stacey told me that she and Mike had made love the previous Tuesday. She grabbed my arm and led me to the bathroom to talk. She was slurring her words and talking about Mike and Patty. Her eyes weren't focusing.*
>
> *I told her that every girl Mike had lived with, he dumped her and got another one to live with. Stacey wanted to know why Mike left her. I told*

her that Mike said she drank too much. "That's very funny coming from him, he's been doing crack for two months," Stacey told me.

I told her, "Don't worry about getting him back." Stacey usually joked, but that night she was depressed. She kept drinking, staring at the floor. Meanwhile, on the other side of the room, Mike was angry, glaring at the wall, hostile-like, mad at the world. I asked him if he was doing drugs.

"No baby," he told me.

I told him Stacey said he had been doing drugs. "Not now, but getting ready to get some," Mike told me.

I told Stacey that Mike said he had not been doing drugs. "That's a lie," she said. Stacey told me she and Mike were supposed to do drugs, or did some, at her apartment that day. She kept talking about Mike, about making love, and about Mike loving her. Mike had calmed down. People were buying Stacey wine coolers. I tried to get her to slow down, that she had had enough.

Cliff Spencer came in and started talking to Mike. They left the bar together and came back in about 10 to 15 minutes. Mike's jaws were locked, and he appeared to be on drugs. He walked over to Stacey, waving his arms. Stacey left the bar crying. I told Mike not to let her leave in that condition alone. He said, "Fuck Stacey." I tried to get a guy to walk her home. He said, "I don't want to get in the middle."

I threw my pool stick on the table and said, "There's not a fucking man in here." I walked out after Stacey, catching her in front of the Duchess of Dare, near her car. We hugged and said goodbye. That would have been about 9:30 p.m. or a few minutes earlier. I walked back to the Green Dolphin. Mike Brandon was still there, and I believe Cliff was too....

Mike had a former girlfriend in Rocky Mount. He beat her. He borrowed money from me to get her an abortion. I loaned him the money, by check. I know he had given her black eyes....

Stacey told me that Mike had hit her, but she gave no description of the assault.

In the past, Mike had beaten a girlfriend and given her black eyes. Stacey told me he had hit her some.

The interview ended at 5:50 p.m., just less than an hour after its start.

Mike Brandon had gone by the Green Dolphin the Sunday after Stacey's body was found, telling a bar employee that he and Stacey had worked things out before she was killed and things had been much better for them. The employee found Brandon's statement "strange."

Shortly thereafter, Mike Brandon's sister, Tina Bass, threatened McGuinness, telling her not to talk about the case, McGuinness told the SBI in a second interview. "It won't be safe for you in Manteo if you keep implying that Mike and Patty had something to do with Stacey's death," Bass told her.

After her interview with the SBI, McGuinness would keep her silence for years before finally breaking it.

—⁂—

THE NEXT DAY, WEDNESDAY, at 11:15 a.m., Lieutenant Colonel Williams interviewed Sherry Collins, a co-worker of Mike Brandon, at the sheriff's office. Collins described Brandon as "volatile" and said he had pulled a knife on two local women on separate occasions but had not cut them. (One of those women, Debra Johnson, would later tell the author she was pregnant when Brandon threatened her, calling her a "c———.") He had beaten a previous girlfriend, Collins said, but said Brandon is "not willing to say he has a temper or does these things."

She said she'd talked with Joni Newman, who owned the house where Brandon and Patty visited around the time Stacey was killed. Joni told her that Brandon and Patty woke her up arguing at about 1:00–1:30 a.m. on February 3, Collins said, and again between 5:30 and 6:00 a.m.

—⁂—

LATER THAT WEEK, TYRRELL County sheriff Roy Brickhouse confirmed to the *Coastland Times* that a man wanted on drug charges in New Jersey was questioned about Stacey's slaying by the SBI and Dare County lawmen Monday in the Tyrrell County jail. "The suspect is from Tyrrell but has friends in Dare County," Brickhouse said. He did not name Spencer.

Nor did the investigators. "We're not at the stage of the investigation to have any suspects," Chief Day told the newspaper.

Yet by that time, the investigators had started to focus on Spencer as the main suspect.

Day said that "the murder weapon had not been found up to that time and investigators did not know what it is, but they were looking for a knife, scissors or sharp object which might have been used to cut the victim's throat," according to the paper.

He added, "Many, many rumors have come back to us regarding this case and some of them are bordering on the ridiculous." He defended the lack of information being released. "The premature release of information can harm the investigation, and we just can't afford to do that. One person knows what has happened, and we don't want to give them anything," Day said.

There was turmoil on the investigative team. "Day, who resigned two weeks ago but reconsidered after town officials agreed to make some operating adjustments to allow him more voice in policy decisions regarding his department, said, 'I left…and I felt like I was 26. Today I think you could turn the numbers around,'" the newspaper reported.

Privately, Day was feeling pressure from Mayor Luther Daniels and Town Commissioner Boyd Midgett, the good friend of Stacey's family, to solve the case. Daniels, brilliant and, at sixty-nine, several years older than Day, served in the U.S. Merchant Marine in World War II, attended Rutgers University and Ohio State University and became a well-respected nuclear engineer before retiring to his island. He was a committed public servant but could get impatient when issues weren't moving fast enough.

Daniels and other local officials knew Stacey and wanted justice for her. They also knew the tourist season was looming, and headlines about a grisly, unsolved murder case would hurt business.

Luther Daniels, mayor of Manteo during the probe of Stacey's killing. *Drew C. Wilson via the Outer Banks History Center, State Archives.*

—◆—

The following Thursday, February 8, the investigative team met in Manteo and discussed the probe. They decided that SBI agents Inscoe, Tony Cummings and Leroy Allen would go to Columbia for another interview with Spencer.

At about 4:00 p.m., Cummings and Allen sat down with Spencer at the Tyrrell County Sheriff's Office. The investigators wrote that they advised Spencer of his rights before the interview began, and he acknowledged that he understood his rights and agreed to talk. Spencer repeated much of what he'd already said about the night at the Green Dolphin in the hours before Stacey's slaying. He added that he had laid down with Stacey on the mattress in her living room in front of the TV and that she had yelled at him that "he was not Mike."

Cummings, a master at playing "the good cop" during interviews, then asked, "Was that when Stacey came at you with a case-cutter knife?"

According to the investigators, Spencer "leaned forward in his chair, put his head down, closed his eyes, and nodded his head 'Yes' two or three times."

That segment of the interview would become hotly contested in the years ahead.

Cummings thanked Spencer for being "honest." Spencer said, "I'm not clear about that part, that part is hazy," according to the SBI file. (Spencer told the author in 2023 that his memory was "hazy," but he was not in a blackout drunk during those hours.)

Spencer told the investigators he wanted to go back to his cell. The interview ended about 4:30 p.m., according to the investigators. The lawmen, after less than a week on the case, were getting impatient. They had been unable to wrench a confession from Spencer. They ramped up their game with a road trip.

—◆—

Almost four hours later, at about 8:00 p.m., the investigators wrote that they asked Spencer if he would ride with them to Manteo, ostensibly so he could tell them the walking route he took on the night Stacey was killed. According to the SBI file, Spencer asked the investigators before they left:

What happens if I am not real clear about some important things? I remember being there with Stacey, then leaving the apartment to talk to Mike. I remember going back to the apartment and lying down with Stacey.

The SBI claimed in their notes that Spencer told them he took off his clothes and lay down on the mattress beside Stacey, but he was "not real clear" about the knife Cummings had asked him about. According to the SBI, Spencer said the reason he was not clear was because he had drunk a lot and used crack cocaine. He was afraid that the things that were hazy would hurt him, the SBI quoted him as saying. The investigators wrote that Spencer told them he was not sure about what happened after "Stacey got upset and got crazy."

"He stated that he used the bathroom and washed his hands before he left Stacey's apartment, and [when] he left 'she was lying sprawled out on the floor,'" the investigators wrote.

They also wrote that Spencer said, "I mean, I don't know about committing a murder, man, what a nightmare."

The investigators loaded Spencer into their car and headed for Manteo. By law, they should have had a judge's order to remove an inmate in the custody of one county sheriff to that of another county, especially since Spencer was being held on the fugitive warrant from New Jersey and he had not been charged in Stacey's slaying.

The investigators said Spencer consented to the ride. Spencer would later say he never consented.

It was a haunted winter night drive of thirty minutes down two-lane 64, past canals by the road and deer, the car headlights catching their eyes eerie red. There were beat-down fishing shacks with broken-down boats in weed-smothered yards. SBI agent Inscoe drove. SBI agent Tony Cummings rode shotgun. Spencer sat in the back seat with agent Allen, ignoring the investigators' questions, pretending to sleep, just a few days past the night when he'd caught a ride into Manteo when it all went bad.

In Manteo, the investigators said, Spencer "voluntarily" showed them the walking route he took in the early morning hours when Stacey was killed, from her apartment to his friend's house where he crashed. When that was done, the investigators drove Spencer to the small airport on the island's North End, where the Dare Sheriff's Department had a satellite office for its drug enforcement team. The department had established the office, in part, one former deputy later said, to protect the confidentiality of their witnesses. Interviewing them at the main office in the courthouse in downtown Manteo just didn't work, he said, with too many bystanders seeing the witnesses coming in and out and adding those sightings to island gossip, inhibiting potential witnesses.

But for Spencer, the secluded nature of the office was chilling, he would later say. He was all alone with the investigators, and his family and lawyer had no idea where he was.

Cummings and Allen interrogated Spencer. This re-creation of parts of that interview is based on the investigators' notes, most of which Spencer would later deny saying:

> *Spencer: The events surrounding Stacey's death were like a videotape playing in my mind. I remember going back to her apartment, seeing her on the floor on the mattress, and getting on it beside her. I took my clothes off and fooled around with her. Then she realized I wasn't Mike, and Stacey kicked me and raised hell with me. Man, I just got foggy. She was loud and crazy.*

He admitted to "losing it" and stabbing a woman in Germany when he was in the army there. The investigators were tracking down Spencer's military records from his time in Germany, finding that he had been convicted of assaulting two women, including one with scissors, and had been incarcerated for a brief period. The investigators sought to tie that to their case against Spencer in Stacey's killing. It was an old police strategy that basically boils down to if the suspect did this, then he could have done the current crime.

Agent Cummings told Spencer that the only thing different about Stacey's killing was that he used a case-cutter knife to kill Stacey. According to the investigators' notes, "Spencer looked down and gave no response to Cummings."

Shortly thereafter, Spencer ended the interview. "I want to go back to the Columbia jail," he said. "I want my attorney present."

Inscoe wrote in his notes that he called the attorney, Charles Ogletree, at his home and that the lawyer agreed to meet his client the next morning at 9:30 at the Columbia jail.

But on the ride back, at about 11:10 p.m., the investigators contended in their notes, "Spencer initiated a conversation."

Spencer had shortly before asked for his lawyer, but the investigators kept interrogating him. He talked about the hazy and foggy part of his fight with Stacey, according to the investigators' notes. As he finished talking, according to the investigators, Spencer added this: "One thing is for sure, I am not a cold-blooded killer. Something must have happened."

If Spencer actually said that, there is no indication in the investigators' notes that they asked him what he meant by "something must have happened." Could he have meant the killer came on Stacey after he left?

The interview ended about 11:40 p.m., the investigators wrote.

Earlier that Thursday, Stacey's death certificate was filed at the Manteo courthouse. It left the time of her death wide open, only stating that it had occurred in "the early AM" of February 3. That lack of specificity was one of the many challenges the investigators faced.

—m—

THE NEXT MORNING, SBI agents Inscoe, Cummings, Allen, Hooks, and Poole; Chief Day; and Lieutenant Colonel Williams met at the Tyrrell County Sheriff's Office in Columbia. The number of investigators in on that meeting suggests that the investigators were concerned that they had been caught in taking Spencer out of Tyrrell County without a judicial order and that they had continued to question him after he had asked for his attorney.

Attorney Ogletree and Spencer's father arrived and conferred with Spencer. After that meeting, Ogletree told the investigators that Spencer said he did not tell the investigators that "Stacey came at him with a knife."

That afternoon, February 9, the investigators drove to the DA's office in Elizabeth City to meet with assistant district attorneys Frank Parrish and Nancy Lamb on the case. The investigators pushed to charge Spencer. "The case was thoroughly related to them," SBI agent Inscoe wrote. "The opinion of both Parrish and Lamb was that there was not sufficient evidence to charge Spencer at that time."

—m—

ON THE AFTERNOON OF Monday, February 12, at 4:55, Agent Inscoe and Chief Day went to the home of Stacey's landlord, Mary Midgett, and interviewed her. Mary, plainspoken and quietly tough, was still grieving her husband, Sam, who had died the year before. She lived in the brick house in front of Stacey's apartment building.

Midgett told the investigators she had not heard "anything suspicious or out of the ordinary" during the time frame when Stacey was killed. Early that Saturday morning, she said, she got up, made coffee and went out on her back porch to read the paper. Apparently, she'd finished reading the paper, wrapped it back up and thrown it toward Stacey's apartment for her to read it.

> *At about 7:30, I saw Mike Brandon walk to the steps of Stacey's apartment, where he picked up her paper and walked it to the top of the steps. I was sure about the time, because I have a clock next to the rear door and looked at it. Mike didn't enter the apartment but put the paper down at the top of the stairs and walked down. He spoke to me as he left.*

Investigators, after interviews with the newspaper deliverer, said that the paper had been delivered about 5:20 a.m. The deliveryman, interviewed by the author in June 2023, could not remember telling the investigators that. Midgett said in a second interview that Stacey did not subscribe to the paper. Midgett said that it had been her custom, for about a year, to read the paper and give it to Stacey.

—⁓—

On February 13 in Manteo, SBI agent Bill Thompson gave Mike Brandon a polygraph test. The test was "inconclusive," Thompson wrote.

Polygraph tests are notoriously unreliable, hence the reason they are inadmissible in court. Polygraph testing has advanced little since its inception in the early twentieth century and is mainly used as a strategic investigative tool—an often unreliable one—by both the state and the defense.

—⁓—

On Friday, February 16, Agents Inscoe and Hooks, Chief Day and Lieutenant Colonel Williams made another trip to the district attorney's office in Elizabeth City to confer on the case. The investigators again pushed to charge Spencer. This time, the head district attorney, H.P. Williams, joined assistant district attorneys Frank Parrish and Nancy Lamb in the meeting. "The case was verbally reviewed again," the agents wrote. "District Attorney Williams advised there was still insufficient evidence to arrest Spencer."

District Attorney H.P. Williams.
Drew C. Wilson via the Outer Banks History Center, State Archives.

On February 20, the investigators made another run at Patty Rowe, Mike Brandon's girlfriend. She said she had met Mike the previous September, when her brother, Ray Griggs, had an apartment adjacent to Stacey's. She had earlier told them she and Brandon didn't start dating until the previous December but now said they had seen each other a couple of times before that, while he was still with Stacey. While Stacey was gone for Christmas and Brandon still had access to Stacey's apartment, Rowe said, she and Brandon spent a night together in the apartment.

Rowe said a bit more about the fight she had with Stacey that she had mentioned in the previous interview. Now, she said, the fight had been soon after Stacey returned from New Jersey after Christmas, and it was in the parking lot in front of Stacey's apartment. She said she "picked up a board" and hit Stacey with it. "Mike broke it up," she said.

Rowe said she had learned on Thursday, February 1, that she was pregnant by Brandon, two days before Stacey's body was found on that Saturday. Brandon "had an idea" she might be pregnant, she said, and he had learned she was from her (Rowe's) mother at the diner.

Although she had said before, that, during the hours when Stacey was killed, Brandon was with her until 9:15 that morning at Joni Newman's apartment, she now said that he had left the apartment alone between 7:00 and 8:00 a.m. that Saturday, asking her if she wanted to go and she said no. He then called the apartment from the Duchess of Dare. When he returned, she said, he had on the same clothes he had worn the previous night. And, in contrast to what Sherry Collins had told investigators, Rowe said she and Brandon had not argued in the early morning hours of Saturday.

> *Investigators: Do you have any idea who killed Stacey?*
> *Rowe: No.*
> *Investigators: Did Mike kill Stacey?*
> *Rowe: No.*
> *Investigators: Did you kill Stacey?*

Rowe: No.

Investigators: Is Mike short-tempered when he drinks?

Rowe: Yea. Me too.

Investigators: Does Mike carry a knife?

Rowe: Yea, pocketknife…

Investigators: Did you ever smoke crack with Cliff?

Rowe: I smoked crack with Cliff. He tried to kiss me. I said no. He wanted to go out with me. [Later, she'd add that was at a trailer where he lived in Manteo.]

Investigators: Did he get aggressive?

Rowe: No. Said I was prejudiced.

Investigators: How was Cliff when he smoked crack?

Rowe: High—paranoid, kept looking out windows.

Investigators: When did you last smoke crack?

Rowe: 10–11 months ago.

THE NEXT AFTERNOON AT the sheriff's office at 3:30, Lieutenant Colonel Williams made one more run at Patty Rowe. This time, in response to questioning, she said that Mike Brandon was upset with her because she was pregnant and she didn't have her driver's license. She was trying to get the license back, she said, and she wouldn't have tried to stop Brandon and Stacey if they wanted to get back together. Regarding the Saturday that Stacey's body was found, Rowe said she got to work at 11:00 a.m., and her boss told her that afternoon that Stacey had been killed. Mike came in the bar about 3:00 or 3:30 that afternoon, she said.

THE FOLLOWING AFTERNOON AT the office, Lieutenant Colonel Williams and Chief Day interviewed Joni Newman about the time frame in which Stacey was killed. Newman said she went to bed about 1:15 a.m. because she had to drive the next morning. Asked if she heard Brandon and Rowe arguing, she said she "could hear voices, not arguing, not yelling." About 5:30 a.m., Newman said, she woke up, noting the time by the clock on her bed. "I went out in the living room [where Brandon and Rowe were], had [a] cigarette and [a] Pepsi….Mike asked if we wanted to go out to the diner for breakfast. I…went back to sleep."

After going to the diner the next morning, Newman said, Brandon called from there about 8:00 a.m.

Newman "was a free spirit, a lover of horses and spending as much time on the beach as she could, especially in collecting sea glass, those wonderous pieces that the ocean transforms from sharp-edged danger to tiny pieces of art," friends would later say. She was a good, fun woman. She also had a history of drug use, as did several of the key witnesses and suspects in the case.

—⁓—

On February 28 at 10:15 a.m. in Columbia, Agent Inscoe, Chief Day and Lieutenant Colonel Williams interviewed Spencer again.

> *Spencer: When I left Stacey that night, she was alive. I believe she was standing in the hall when I left....* [Before that] *I had gone to sleep beside Stacey. She nudged me with her right foot and said, "You're not Mike" but she was not mad and she said it in a calm voice.*
>
> *I'm tired of talking. I have nothing else to say. Everything I've said I've already said before.*

In handwritten notes, Inscoe wrote, "Cliff appeared nervous, hands shaking clasp hands [*sic*] together drawn in towards lap when talking about Stacey's pants and how she was she last seen." The investigators wrote that they ended the interview at 11:20 a.m.

—⁓—

As the probe continued, Stacey's mother kept calling Manteo officials for updates. "It was all hush-hush," Ed Stanton Jr. said. "My mom was a retired civil service worker and knew how to push all the right buttons. But she wasn't getting anywhere, even with the help of Boyd Midgett."

The investigators cleared Mike Brandon, believing that Joni Newman's statement gave him an alibi. Given her history of drug abuse, it's questionable that the investigators relied on her as the key witness to alibi Brandon.

—⁓—

On March 1 in Dare County, SBI agent Bill Thompson met with Patty Rowe, Brandon's girlfriend, to give her a polygraph test. The test "was stopped due to the fact that [she] became sick prior to the test, possibly as a result of her being pregnant at the time of the test," according to the SBI file.

Rowe told the lawmen she would take the test at a later date, she told the author in April 2023, but no one ever called her.

Chief Day made his final exit the next week. On Wednesday, March 7, the town board, on a motion by Boyd Midgett, voted to accept Day's resignation "and write him a letter of thanks." Day resigned "over what he said was meddling in the investigation by Mayor Luther H. Daniels," the *Virginian-Pilot* newspaper reported. In later action, the board would unanimously vote to deny Day payment "for annual leave, sick leave or extra hours worked."

That same day, March 7, in a letter to Lieutenant Colonel Williams of the Dare Sheriff's Department, perhaps sent by fax, the SBI dropped a bombshell: no "Negroid hair" had been found on Stacey's body, based on the hair samplings Agent Honeycutt had sent them.

D.T. Hamlin of the SBI wrote that Agent Dennis Honeycutt had submitted hairs from Stacey's right and left hands, her chest, her mouth and pubic area. He wrote that "examination" of those items "did not reveal any Negroid hair."

Hamlin continued: "Per communication with S/A I.K. Inscoe the remainder of the evidence need not be examined for a hair transfer."

Why didn't Inscoe ask for further examination when it could have revealed another suspect?

As it was, the investigators and DA Williams were pursuing a murder case against a Black defendant with no "Negroid" hairs on the white victim's body.

The next day, March 8, SBI supervisor Bill Godley told Agent Inscoe that DA Williams had authorized a warrant for first-degree murder to be sworn out against Spencer and that investigators should prepare to eventually drive to New Jersey to pick up Spencer, where he was being held on the drug charge. The SBI file does not indicate what prompted the decision to charge Spencer, given that, the previous month, DA Williams had said there was not enough evidence for a charge.

In a June 2023 phone call with the author, former DA Williams declined to comment on the case.

In addition to the timing of the SBI report, the fact that Day's resignation was accepted one day before Godley said DA Williams authorized charging Spencer is intriguing, especially since Day had alleged meddling in the case by Mayor Daniels and that Spencer had found Day to be the most sympathetic officer on his case. Day once said privately that he felt sorry for Spencer after the last interview he did with him. He did not say whether he felt Spencer was guilty or innocent.

———

AT A MARCH 13, 1990 press conference at the Manteo Town Hall, investigators announced that Spencer would be charged, naming him publicly for the first time. SBI supervisor Godley revealed little. He said, "There was reason to believe the victim was acquainted with Spencer," according to the *Coastland Times*. "Part of the case rests on physical evidence, he said, and a drug connection has been suggested." He did not elaborate on either point.

He said the defendant "chose not to be represented by an attorney when he was questioned in Columbia." Yet Charles Ogletree was present with Spencer a few times during the questioning in Columbia, according to the SBI's own notes. Godley failed to mention that Spencer had requested an attorney when he was interviewed on Roanoke Island but was not provided one.

———

AS MARCH CONTINUED, THE investigators interviewed Ray Griggs, Patty Rowe's brother, who had lived in the apartment beside Stacey before he left the apartment and Marty Madden moved in. On March 28, Lieutenant Colonel Jasper Williams interviewed Griggs at the sheriff's office. According to Williams's handwritten notes, Griggs had lived in the apartment about a year and had moved out about three or four months before her killing. The walls of the apartment were thin, he said. He remembered seeing Stacey in the Green Dolphin the Friday night before she was killed. His sister, Patty, was there, he said, as was Mike Brandon and Cliff. Stacey, Griggs said, was apparently upset, "a little high, leaning on the jukebox." Stacey made overtures to Brandon, Griggs said, and Brandon told her, "I wish you would go ahead and leave." Cliff was "on something—drugs," Griggs said.

Between 1:30 and 1:45 a.m. on Saturday, Griggs said, he rode his bike over to Joni Newman's house, where Brandon and Patty had allegedly gone, and met Cathy Rogers there, who had just driven up. They knocked on the door, he said, but there was no answer. Griggs added: "I saw Mike later in the day between 3–4 p.m. and he told me Stacey was dead. He was a totally different person." The SBI file does not indicate what Griggs meant by "totally different person."

—m—

ALSO IN MARCH, THE investigators interviewed Spencer's former Columbia jail-mates, seeking incriminatory statements he might have made to them.

Many a defendant has been convicted in varying degrees on jailhouse informant statements. These informants are notorious for embellishment, often lying about those statements and even making up statements to gain favor on their own cases.

The interviews yielded little of substance, with Spencer having said little or nothing about his case. It's telling that none of the jailhouse interviews in Spencer's case yielded incriminating information. In fact, the jailhouse informant interviews in Spencer's case were largely in his

Cliff Spencer arriving for an initial court appearance in Manteo. *Drew C. Wilson via the Outer Banks History Center, State Archives.*

favor. There is no indication in the records that any of the informants gained lenient treatment for information they told investigators about what Spencer told them.

On April 2, 1990, a Dare County grand jury indicted Spencer on a charge of first-degree murder in Stacey's death. Three witnesses presented evidence in the private proceedings: Lieutenant Colonel Williams, Agent Inscoe and former chief Day.

—⁓—

ON THURSDAY, MAY 31, Lieutenant Colonel Williams and Agent Inscoe drove up to Salem, New Jersey, to pick up Spencer, who pleaded guilty to the cocaine charge and waived an extradition fight. The lawmen signed him out of the Salem jail at about 10:30 a.m. and loaded him into their car. Williams drove, and Inscoe sat in the backseat with Spencer. About 10:45 a.m., as they crossed the Delaware River bridge, Inscoe read Spencer his rights. Spencer said he would talk to them but had already said what he was going to say. Inscoe wrote that they engaged in general conversation, and Spencer did not make any incriminating statements. "Spencer did say that he was going to hire his own attorney, that he had employed a lawyer in Greensboro [North Carolina]," Inscoe wrote. "Spencer further advised that he was not going to plead to anything, that he wanted a trial."

They arrived at the Manteo courthouse that night. Lieutenant Colonel Williams read Spencer his rights. The lawmen charged Spencer with first-degree murder in Stacey's death and placed him in the Manteo jail.

Dare County officials later moved Spencer to Central Prison in Raleigh "for safekeeping."

On June 12, 1990, Spencer was transported from Raleigh to Manteo for his arraignment. Represented by defense attorney Romallus Murphy of Greensboro, he entered a not guilty plea in Dare County Superior Court. Assistant district attorney Nancy Lamb said the state would seek the death penalty.

10

A "Legendary" Lawyer

So I want to know how long do you think I would have to stay in here before I go to trial or you get some information from the prosecutor.
—*Cliff Spencer in an August 16, 1990 letter to Romallus Murphy*

Spencer's family was apprehensive about having a court-appointed attorney out of Dare County represent him. There were few, if any, Black lawyers in the county on the local court-appointed list, much less any with experience in death penalty cases. Spencer's family decided to raise funds to retain a lawyer for Spencer. Through friends, they learned of Romallus Murphy in Greensboro, in the central part of North Carolina. His record was impressive.

A Houston native, Murphy was a sixty-two-year-old graduate of Howard University in Washington, D.C., one of the country's premier historically Black universities. He was an air force veteran, having been honorably discharged as a captain. He completed his undergraduate studies at Howard, started law school there and finished at the University of North Carolina School of Law, where he was the only student of color when he graduated in 1956.

He hung out his shingle in Wilson, North Carolina, where he said he was the only Black attorney in that part of eastern North Carolina. In 1959, he brought a voting lawsuit against the City of Wilson. He fought the case all the way up to the U.S. Supreme Court. His supporters said the case, though unsuccessful, helped persuade Congress to pass the Voting

Rights Act of 1965. He had served as chairman of the Legal Redress Committee of the North Carolina Conference of the NAACP since the 1960s and had served as legal counsel to the North Carolina conference. He'd been part of a legal team that had forced North Carolina to establish legal opportunities for Black lawyers to become superior court judges. Some even called Murphy a living legend.

The Spencer family, impressed by his experience, retained him in June 1990, agreeing to pay him $20,000 for Cliff's defense (about $46,000 in 2023 dollars), money they started to raise in their community. Spencer and his family began calling Murphy the "NAACP lawyer."

Murphy visited with Spencer at Central Prison in Raleigh and had telephone chats with Spencer's mother. But then, Murphy became harder to reach.

Spencer wrote, in an August 16 letter to Murphy,

> Mr. Murphy, what I am getting at is this: I don't want to have to sit here in the prison for another 5 or 6 months and still don't know anything. I know you can only do but so much and I know you will be honest with me. So I want to know how long do you think I would have to stay in here before I go to trial or you get some information from the prosecutor.

—⁓—

Spencer was unaware of the March 7 letter to Lieutenant Colonel Williams of the Dare Sheriff's Department from the SBI lab that no "Negroid hair" had been found on Stacey's body, based on the hair samplings Agent Honeycutt had sent them.

Murphy should have been fighting to see those lab results. But he did nothing. Spencer had no way of knowing that. But he was beginning to sense his lawyer was slack.

In a letter to Murphy dated September 15, Spencer wrote:

> The reason why I am writing you is because it has been over a month since I last wrote you and I still haven't gotten any answer from my last letter. Mr. Murphy, I would like to know what is going on out there. There has been enough time passed for the prosecutor to have given you something. Please write me back and let me know something.

Murphy did not respond.

—m—

ON SEPTEMBER 5, 1990, Mike Brandon and Patty Rowe married. Three days later, Patty gave birth to their baby boy.

Mike Brandon's criminal activity had accelerated, including burglaries, assaults on law enforcement officers and, in one notorious incident in June 1990, the larceny of a boat. Jimmy Ray Watts, who worked the case as a Nags Head police officer, said they received a report of a stolen boat on "Pond Island," in the Roanoke Sound off the Causeway. Watts and his partner spotted Brandon and a friend trying to start a boat. When they saw the lawmen, Brandon and his friend jumped in the water to swim away. The lawmen commandeered another boat and dragged in Brandon and his friend, easily subduing the friend. Brandon was a different story. For the next several hours, Watts said, he and his partner fought to keep Brandon, who was clearly coked out, in custody. They wrestled and exchanged fist hits, Watts said, with Brandon having the strength of ten men, before they finally subdued and jailed him.

Years later, Watts said, he saw Brandon and asked him what he was thinking that night. "I just wanted to see if you all could beat me," Brandon told him. Watts told him: "You gave us a run."

I asked Watts if Brandon could have killed Stacey. "Absolutely," he said.

11

"Mrs. Spencer, They Want to Kill Your Son"

Mrs. Spencer, they want to kill your son.... The state really doesn't have anything on him, but he talked too much, making incriminating statements.
—Romallus Murphy to Cliff Spencer's parents in December 1990

District attorney H.P. Williams had apparently not given his full concentration to the case. While he had at times told the investigators concentrating on Spencer to go back and get him hard evidence, he seemed distracted. At least one of his assistant district attorneys, Nancy Lamb, had serious doubts about the evidence against Spencer. At Williams's request, Lamb had represented the state at Spencer's arraignment hearing the previous June, saying the state would seek the death penalty. But even then, she'd had doubts about the case, and those doubts had mounted. Lamb, a rising star in the district attorney's office, had decided that she would have nothing else to do with the case and confront her boss on it he pressed her to stay involved.

Williams obviously sensed weakness in Murphy. In a phone chat on December 4, 1990, Williams told Murphy that in exchange for Cliff's guilty plea, the charge against him would be reduced to second-degree murder and he would be sentenced life in prison. The death penalty would be off the table. In a follow-up letter to Murphy dated December 7—the anniversary of the Japanese attack on Pearl Harbor—Williams wrote, "This offer remains open until the January 7, 1991, session of Criminal Superior Court in Dare County."

Williams had just released to Murphy the state's discovery evidence—its summary of its case against Spencer—at the end of November. Good defense lawyers take months, sometime years, to wade through discovery, finding weaknesses in the state's case and witnesses. But Murphy was sloppy, and Williams knew it. Williams did not alert Murphy to the fact, in the discovery, that no "Negroid" hairs had been found on Stacey's body. It was Murphy's job to find that, but some prosecutors do alert defense attorneys to such discrepancies, especially when the defense lawyer is lacking.

Instead, Williams played high-stakes poker with Spencer's future, giving Murphy one month to play or fold, with the emotional holiday season unfolding.

—⁂—

December 1990 was a hard Christmas season for Spencer in Central Prison in Raleigh. Murphy, despite the money Spencer's parents had agreed to pay him, had done little on the case, not once going to the crime scene, conferring with investigators or interviewing potential witnesses. Instead, Murphy spent much of his time on the phone with his client's mom, telling her that the odds were against her son as a Black man charged with killing a white girl in a southern town. "Mrs. Spencer, they want to kill your son," he told Spencer's mother more than once.

If the case went to trial, he said, Spencer would be convicted and get "the electric chair." North Carolina had not used the chair in decades for capital punishment, having moved to letting the condemned choose the gas chamber or lethal injection by the time of Cliff's case. Almost all chose lethal injection.

Murphy made a rare visit to see Spencer in Central Prison in December. He told his client about the discovery materials, specifically the statements Spencer had allegedly made to investigators. "You are in trouble," Murphy told Spencer. "There is nothing I can do for you."

Spencer pushed back, saying that the statements weren't true and noting that he had never signed them or written any of them.

"It doesn't make any difference," Murphy told. "That's what the SBI is going to get up there and say that you did. There's no way in the world you can win this case. I can get you a plea."

Spencer told his lawyer, "I'm not going to accept no f—— plea and I don't want a plea."

District Attorney H.P. Williams on his way to a court appearance. *Drew C. Wilson via the Outer Banks History Center, State Archives.*

—⁂—

DURING THE CHRISTMAS HOLIDAYS, one of Cliff's sisters, Karen, and his parents visited Spencer in Central Prison. As much as he appreciated his family visiting him, he was embarrassed for them to have to see him there.

Before the visit, Spencer's family met with Murphy for breakfast at a Shoney's restaurant in Raleigh. Between bites in the crowded room, Murphy told them he had received the discovery. "It doesn't look very good for Cliff," Murphy said. "He won't stand a chance if he appears in court, the things that he said. The state really doesn't have anything on him, but he talked too much, making incriminating statements."

Murphy never mentioned that those statements could be suppressed, given that Spencer had never signed them and his consent to them was questionable.

Instead, he again expressed concern about the racial aspect of the case. "Cliff being a Black man, he wouldn't stand a chance."

Then he told them about the district attorney's offer. "Talk to your son, and, if possible, persuade him to enter a plea," Murphy told them.

Murphy never mentioned the SBI finding about the lack of "Negroid" hairs found on Stacey's body and SBI agent Kent Inscoe's decision not to ask for further findings—if Murphy had even read that in the discovery.

In the weeks ahead, Murphy accelerated his push on Spencer's parents and Spencer for him to enter a plea. Spencer continued to say he would not plead guilty to a crime he did not commit. Murphy sent Spencer's mother to see him in his jail cell. She cried and told him to take the plea bargain. Murphy had told her that, because of prison overcrowding, Cliff would be out in seven years. But Spencer remained firm. He told his mother, once more, that he would not enter a plea.

12

THE BLEAK SURPRISE IN MANTEO

January 8, 1991

Lawyers stopping by the Manteo courtroom could not believe what they saw.

On January 8, 1991, Romallus Murphy had a motions hearing scheduled at the Manteo courthouse. The motions he had filed included a request for a change of venue "on the grounds that the defendant cannot obtain a fair and impartial trial in [Dare] county" and a request for the disclosure of other suspects in the state's investigation. It soon became apparent that Murphy had other action in mind.

Spencer had been brought to the Manteo jail, adjacent to the courthouse, from Central Prison the day before, wanting to go ahead with the motions. But he was caving under Murphy's relentless pressure. On the night of January 7, he telephoned his ex-wife in Germany. She cried, scared that Cliff would get the death penalty. Cliff could hear his daughter crying as well. At three and a half, she was far too young to know what was going on. But she knew her mother was upset, so she was as well. And that, in turn, upset Spencer.

Early the next morning, Murphy met with Spencer's mother, then visited Spencer in the Manteo jail. Murphy laid out some of the discovery papers, but far from all. The main thing Murphy showed his client was SBI summaries of the statements the investigators said Cliff had made to them.

Murphy: You can't win. You will lose your life if you go to court like this.
Spencer: Mr. Murphy, I can't plead guilty to something I never done.
Murphy: Well, you can plead nolo contendere.
Spencer: What's that?
Murphy: No contest. Let me go talk to DA Williams. I'll be right back.

In no contest pleas, defendants acknowledge that the state has enough evidence to secure a conviction but do not admit guilt. These pleas give defendants a bit of help in appeals but not much. They do give defendants who maintain their innocence a certain peace of mind.

Murphy soon returned from the district attorney's office with a plea agreement filled out, including the no contest plea. Spencer lingered over the document, fighting within himself over what he should do. Ultimately, haunted by the words from his mother and his ex-wife and his daughter's crying and not wanting to be exposed to the threat of execution, Spencer signed. Now came the hearing.

—⁂—

THE COURTHOUSE WAS AROUND the corner from the Green Dolphin pub where all the trouble had started and a couple of blocks over from Stacey's apartment, where it had ended. From the front of the courthouse building, you can see Shallowbag Bay, with rich people's yachts docked, ready to sail out to the Roanoke Sound and beyond.

In the wood-paneled courtroom on the second floor of the courthouse, bailiffs escorted Cliff in. Eleven months ago, he'd rolled into Manteo from Columbia on a rocking Friday night, a free man in a free land. Now, he was about to give up his freedom.

As always in Manteo, the island grapevine was working, in this case, spreading the word that a plea was in the offing. Several lawyers not connected to the case stopped by the courtroom to see what would happen.

Superior court judge Herbert "Herb" Small of Elizabeth City called the court to order. Small, sixty-four, had earned his undergraduate degree from the University of Virginia, then served in the navy in World War II and earned his law degree from the University of North Carolina at Chapel Hill. He started out in private practice, then served as district attorney for his area before winning election to the bench.

Judge Small, the district attorney and the investigators were well acquainted and shared mutual respect. Murphy could never have entered their club. He

Cliff Spencer, headed for a court appearance with Lieutenant Colonel Jasper Williams of the Dare County Sheriff's Office. *Drew C. Wilson via the Outer Banks History Center, State Archives.*

could have charmed and cajoled his way close to them in investigating his client's case, as countless out-of-town defense attorneys do, relying on the law to push back when needed, but he hadn't even tried.

Spencer sat grim at the defense table with Murphy by his side. Williams sat across the aisle to their right, at the prosecutor's table. District attorneys, often weighing political considerations, carefully choose which cases they will personally appear in court on, often leaving prosecution and plea hearings to their assistants. Williams chose to handle this one himself.

Judge Small asked Spencer a series of questions aimed at discerning that he understood the plea he was making and was satisfied with his lawyer's services. Spencer answered yes and then entered his plea of no contest.

Judge Small made sure that Spencer understood his plea could result in him being imprisoned for life.

Spencer affirmed he understood.

DA Williams then summarized the state's case, starting by calling SBI agent Dennis Honeycutt to the stand. He described the crime scene. In the bathroom, he said, was "evidence of blood being around the sink, the basin."

District Attorney H.P. Williams during a court hearing. *Drew C. Wilson via the Outer Banks History Center, State Archives.*

Williams: As if someone had washed up?
Honeycutt: Yes sir.
Williams: And in fact, some fingerprints of the defendant were found in the residence?
Honeycutt: They were.

Spencer had repeatedly said he had been in Stacey's apartment and may have left fingerprints. For that matter, the SBI had also found in the apartment the fingerprints of Mike Brandon, who had told the agents he had been in the apartment the Tuesday before Stacey's body was found. In questioning by Williams, Honeycutt never said that Spencer's prints were found in the bathroom blood—they weren't—just that his fingerprints were "found in the residence."

Williams presented photos of the crime scene, including those of Stacey's body.

Next to testify was SBI agent Kent Inscoe. Williams asked him, "At first, who did the investigation focus on?"

Inscoe replied, "The investigation first had focused, first focused on associates and an ex-boyfriend by the name of Mike Brandon. Brandon was interviewed, and, by alibi witnesses, was alibied. The investigation then focused on associates and people that had last been seen with the victim. "

Murphy had never investigated Brandon's alibi.

Inscoe, in replies to questions from Williams, said, in effect, the investigators had zeroed in on Spencer "as he was probably the last person we knew Stacey to be with that night."

Investigators had spoken with him on February 4, 5, 7 "and several other occasions," Inscoe said. On February 4, Inscoe testified, Spencer "never asked us how she was killed....We asked him one time did he carry a gun—he stated that he didn't—anticipating he would ask us if she had been shot.

"We later asked him if he carried a knife. He said he didn't—anticipating that he would ask if she had been stabbed. He never asked us during that initial interview how she died or what was the cause of her death. When we left him at the conclusion of the interview, he had never asked us how she died or anything about her death."

Inscoe testified about the February 8 interview with Spencer done by SBI agents Tony Cummings and Leroy Allen at the Columbia jail. Inscoe said he "was in the next room but could overhear the interview. In this particular interview, he made what we felt was some incriminating statements."

Inscoe continued: "During the interview, Agent Cummings asked at one point, 'Did Stacey come at you with a case-cutter knife?' And Agent Cummings said that Mr. Spencer put his head down and nodded in the affirmative several times."

If there was a one-way window in the Columbia interview room and/or an acoustic connection, Inscoe did not indicate that in his testimony, only that he "could overhear."

Murphy did not raise an objection to the acoustics or to the visuals.

Inscoe went on, testifying about the controversial ride the law enforcement agents had made with Cliff from the Columbia jail to Manteo and the ensuing conversations. Murphy raised no objections.

"I was in the car with Agent Cummings and Agent Allen….During that night that he was interviewed more in my presence, "He [Spencer] also made some other statements that we felt were incriminating," Inscoe testified.

> Williams said, "Go ahead."
>
> Inscoe said, "He had told us—at the time he asked us one question, 'What happens if I am not clear about other important things?' He again stated that he was not sure about what happened after Stacey got upset and crazy. And he had told us that during the night he had come back to the apartment after trying to purchase some crack cocaine, that she was on the mattress in the floor of the living room and that he laid down beside her and that she woke up—that he woke up and she was kicking him in the side, stating 'You are not Mike. You are not Mike,' referring to her boyfriend.
>
> "He stated she went—his exact words were, 'Stacey kicked me and raised hell with me.' And he says, 'Man, I just got foggy. She was loud and crazy.' He also made a statement during this time that—he said that he used the bathroom and washed his hands before he left. And he said that when he left her that her pants were off, that the only thing she had on was this top, and that the last time her she was sprawled—and he used the word 'sprawled'—she was sprawled out on the floor."
>
> Williams: "And that's just how you found her, is it not?"
>
> Inscoe: "Yes sir, it is, yes sir."

Inscoe testified that the murder weapon was not recovered but suggested that it was believed to be a box cutter blade. He noted that Spencer had a misdemeanor cocaine conviction in New Jersey and the two assault convictions while serving with the army in Germany.

Then Williams said, "Your honor, that would be the state's showing."

Murphy said there would be no evidence for the defendant.

Judge Small said, "The court determines that there is a factual basis for the entry of the plea....Mr. Murphy, you said there is no evidence. Is there any showing or statement you wish to make on his behalf before I enter judgment?"

Murphy mentioned the threat of the death penalty in having recommended to his client that he accept the plea. "We can only hope that this encounter was the last encounter of this nature, and to subsequent events," he said. "We think that there are those circumstances in this person's background to indicate that he is salvageable. And we think these circumstances will give him the opportunity to get his life together and make some meaningful contribution to society.

"His mother and father are here and other relatives, and they have been in close contact. So, he does have the family support that one needs in order to sustain himself and overcome a background that certainly has been influenced by the use of drugs, unfortunately. We've got some indication there was use of drugs on this occasion. He's used drugs in other occasions of his life, in other convictions.

"And we looked at all of these circumstances. We thought in our judgment this would be an appropriate resolution of this matter....I think, your Honor, we are hopeful that, at least, that society and time will prove us right, that he indeed will make some contribution to society and cause him to get his life together. We think that all the circumstances are right for him to do just that."

Murphy noted that his associate counsel, David Dansby of Greensboro, had worked on the case. While Murphy was privately retained, Dansby had been appointed by the state. North Carolina requires two attorneys on death penalty cases.

Judge Small said, "All right. Thank you. Ask your client to stand."

Spencer stood, his arms crossed across his chest.

Small said, "It is the judgment of the court that the defendant be confined in the state prison for the rest of his natural life....Sheriff, he's in your custody."

Spencer glanced once more at his family as a bailiff led him out of the courtroom. His mother told him she loved him.

The local defense lawyers who'd come to watch the hearing couldn't believe it. What the hell was that they just saw? They asked each other. Yes, they acknowledged, the photos of Stacey's slashed body, allegedly killed by a Black man, would have inflamed a jury that may well have been predominantly white. But the evidence presented was as flimsy as a torn sail in a nor'easter. Any of them could have taken that case to trial and won, they told themselves, or at the very least, gotten a lesser plea, perhaps to manslaughter, and a far lesser sentence. Only fingerprints tied Spencer to the crime scene, and he had admitted being there. District attorney Williams never mentioned the many other fingerprints that could have been found in the apartment from the numerous bystanders trampling through.

The statements Spencer allegedly gave investigators came after big questions on whether he had surrendered his Miranda rights before he gave the statements. Competent defense attorneys could easily have challenged the statements and perhaps suppressed them, especially those given when he was driven from the Columbia jail to Manteo and back.

Ultimately, in the absence of physical evidence beyond the fingerprints, the state's case had boiled down to the investigators' assertion that when they asked Spencer if Stacey had come at him with a knife, he bowed his head and nodded.

Stacey's family was not in the courtroom, given the sudden switch from a motions hearing to a plea hearing. District Attorney Williams called them with the news. The plea brought no closure to his mother, Ed Stanton Jr. said in 2023, since she thought Mike Brandon was the killer. His father's feelings were different, he said. "He just felt relieved. He was sick and tired of it. He just wanted it to be over." One of Stacey's cousins, Cathy Groves, said in 2023 that Stacey's parents called her and other relatives to their house to tell them about the conviction. They were subdued, suppressing their pain, she said, just saying that a man had been convicted, without expressing any feelings about whether the conviction was justified.

Spencer was crushed, as he realized how weak the state's case had really been and that his lawyer had never told him that. He had just given up his life for nothing. It was smoke and mirrors. For example, SBI agent Inscoe had testified that one indicator of Spencer's guilt was that he never asked the investigators how Stacey had been killed, whether she was shot or stabbed. Spencer knew the answer. He had not needed to ask, because, while he was waiting in the Tyrrell County Sheriff's Office for his first interview with the investigators, he had seen the crime scene photos on a desk.

Although Murphy sat by Spencer during the hearing, Murphy's silence at key points spoke volumes. Spencer may as well have sat at the defense table alone.

Outside the courtroom, Murphy noted to Spencer's father that a "life sentence" allowed for the possibility of parole. "The most time that he would pull is between eight to ten, and then he would be eligible for parole," Murphy told Harry Spencer. "The DA and I talked about it, and they had to give the people something to satisfy them."

No one spoke out. The defense lawyers had to keep dealing with Williams, working out plea agreements for their clients.

Murphy acted like district attorney Williams had given him a gift with the plea. Yet Murphy told reporters that Spencer never confessed to the murder. "He never did indicate to me he did it," Murphy said. "Those are things in the recesses of his own mind."

In its edition the next day, the *Virginia-Pilot* reported the plea. District attorney Williams said: "There is no evidence he [Cliff] planned the murder."

So, on what evidence had Williams initially pursued the death penalty, which requires premeditation?

Williams added that Spencer's "life sentence" for second-degree murder meant he would be eligible for parole in ten years. But there surely was no guarantee.

The newspaper, in its reporting of the plea, erroneously reported, "Investigators found Spencer's bloody fingerprints on a bathroom sink, where it appeared he had tried to wash up after the murder, Inscoe said." Honeycutt, not Inscoe, had been the agent testifying about the crime scene, and Honeycutt never said in the hearing that Spencer's bloody fingerprints were found at the sink, only that Spencer's fingerprints were in the apartment.

Among those following the plea was Buddy Tillett, a road deputy with Dare County. Although he was not assigned to the probe into Stacey's death, Tillett had worked Mike Brandon on drug cases. Brandon was a confidential informant, or "CI," for Tillett, giving him names of who was moving cocaine to gain favor for himself, Brandon. Tillett is short and charismatically coiled, with a quick smile and light storytelling style that belies his tenacity.

Brandon had always given Tillett a bad feeling. He was stone-cold mean in Tillett's view, known as "a knife man" quick to pull his blade. Tillett wondered if Brandon had been involved in Stacey's killing. One day, shortly after the slaying, Tillett asked Brandon if had killed Stacey. Brandon told Tillett he had not killed her.

Tillett was not alone in suspecting Brandon. One of the men in the Green Dolphin on Stacey's last night there confirmed to me that Brandon was a knife man. That white man said he'd met Brandon some time before and distanced himself from him because Brandon was fond of calling Blacks "niggers" and talked of pulling knives on them. "Tina Bass, Mike's sister introduced me to him," he said. "Brandon started talking that trash, and I cut him off for good."

Deputy Terri Williams, one of the first responders to the crime scene, remembered that, on the afternoon Bass had come upon Stacey's body, she told Williams that she hoped her brother, Mike Brandon, hadn't done that. Williams told her she hoped so, too.

Spencer would later wonder at how calm Bass seemed to be in her interview with the investigators about discovering the body. It was almost, he said, like she had expected to find it.

Buddy Tillett, who worked suspect Mike Brandon as a confidential informant on drug cases when Tillett was a Dare County deputy. *Courtesy Buddy Tillett.*

Williams also remembered that, hours after Stacey's body was discovered, Brandon told her that no one needed to see Stacey looking like that. Williams wondered how Brandon would have known how her body looked and told Lieutenant Colonel Jasper Williams. He shrugged her question off, she said. Brandon may have heard from his sister, Tina. But Brandon's statement still bothered Terri Williams. And Brandon's interviews with the investigators should have raised questions about when his sister had talked to him. He had told the lawmen that he hadn't heard Stacey had been killed until he got to the Green Dolphin the afternoon her body was found. Why hadn't he seen the crime-scene crowd outside Stacey's apartment, a few blocks over from the pub, and why wouldn't his sister have told him earlier about finding the body?

Several other locals were bothered by the outcome of the case. Wayne Morris, who alibied Spencer in the early morning hours of February 3, was in the courtroom and shocked by Spencer's plea. "Cliff didn't kill that girl," Morris told the author in July 2023.

Another person bothered by the outcome of the case was a local tree worker who'd known Stacey and knew Mike Brandon. On separate occasions, he told the author, Brandon had pulled a knife on him and a gun, once at Stacey's apartment. "She wanted to get the hell away from him," he said. "He was always going around saying he wanted to kill somebody or some shit. F—— nutjob." The tree worker was pretty handy with his fists, and Brandon backed down. "Mike was a bully badass," he said. He told law enforcement officers, but they never charged Brandon with threatening him.

Stacey told him that if something happened to her, Mike would have done it. He said he told investigators that after Stacey was killed.

Yoyo Daniels, who had let Stacey babysit her children, was also incredulous. "Cliff was a sweet guy and not a killer," she said. These were stories Spencer's lawyer had never pursued.

—⁂—

REALIZING HOW WEAK THE state's case had been, Spencer cried, the only time he did, in his cell in the Manteo jail. The next day, a bailiff shackled him and loaded him into a van for shipment back to Central Prison in Raleigh, where prisoners sent to the state prison go for processing being assigned to prison units throughout the state. The van's windows were heavily screened, preventing Spencer from seeing the fields, forests and waters he was leaving behind as the van headed west. The first night in Central, with the threat of sexual assault, is often a terror to new admittees. But Spencer had been held there awaiting trial. He was big and tough enough to defend himself. His fellow inmates left him alone.

Meanwhile, at the end of January, the North Carolina State Bar reprimanded Murphy for, essentially, not keeping his clients informed on a civil case.

Around the same time, Spencer's mother, Emma, received a letter from Murphy, the first one he had written her. It was a bill for $6,000 for his "work." The family somehow raised the money to pay him. But they were not happy.

Later, Spencer wrote that "the person that I thought was trying to help me only was interested in a paycheck. My family went into debt so I could have legal representation. All we got was a 'greedy old man' who did not care anything about the truth."

Sometime after Cliff's plea, an assistant clerk in the Dare County Courthouse saw Mike Brandon there and told him, "You killed Stacey, and we know you did it." Brandon replied, "No I didn't."

A co-worker told the clerk to shut up or Brandon would kill her, too.

PART III

FIGHTING BACK

—⟋⟍—

NORTH CAROLINA, 1991–2024

13

SPENCER'S APPEAL

Harnett Correctional Institution, Lillington, North Carolina, January 1991 through April 1992

> *When I left the apartment, Stacey Stanton was alive.*
> —*Cliff Spencer in his 1992 motion for appropriate relief*

Cliff was transferred from Central Prison to Harnett Correctional Institution, in southeastern North Carolina, a drive of several hours from his northeastern North Carolina home. He sat in his cell, photos of his family pasted on the cold stone wall. He got bitter. He got mad. And like many inmates, he began to try to live in his head, dreaming of the world outside the prison walls.

He thought back on his life as the oldest of seven children in Columbia, two boys and five girls. He had looked out for his siblings. His father, Harry, worked in a sawmill and, later, for the state ferry service. His mother, Emma, was a homemaker. Cliff dreamed of being an entertainer or a pro athlete. He shot a lot of basketball and played sandlot football. He'd later remember:

> *I wasn't a model child growing up. I used to do little things that my mom would punish me for.…When I first started school, it was like being home-schooled. Most of the teachers were related to the family as they had taught my mother or father. My first five years in school were before schools were integrated and all the Blacks attended* [their own school] *grades 1 to 12.…1969 was the year that schools integrated. To that point I had limited contact with whites. The first day of school I was assigned to sit*

behind this white boy....We developed a friendship that we continue to this day. I started to go around to his house which wasn't far from where I live, we started to get into a lot of stuff as kids and even though my family never said anything to me about my friendship with him, the Black community had a lot to say. In 1970 or '71, we used to break into houses to steal guns to sell.

All of the homes we broke into were in the white neighborhood; and that really did not look good, a Black kid roaming into white neighborhoods late at night with a couple of white kids. My parents never said anything about [my friend] *being white and influencing me, my mother talked to him like he was her son when she saw him, even though there was a lot of talk in the Black community about my friendship. When I finally went to court* [for the break-ins] *I was placed on probation since I attended school regularly. The judge told me he hoped I had learned my lesson. At the time I thought I had but I hadn't.*

In 1973, Cliff's freshman year, he made the junior varsity football team, starting as an end. But at six feet, two inches tall and only 150 pounds, he wasn't strong enough and spent most of his time on the bench. He started playing in the high school band, playing saxophone. And that year, he began experimenting with alcohol and drugs, he and his white friend getting "bums off the street" to buy them gin. They smoked pot because cocaine was too expensive.

That summer it seemed that my relationship with my mom started to deteriorate. It seemed to me that she was much harder on me than the rest of my family. I was her firstborn and now I see it as she only wanted me to do better, she wanted for me what I should have wanted for myself. I think that was the first time in my life that my father ever lost his temper with me. I got my share of beatings growing up for things that I had done. I don't believe it was abusive. When I was a kid, if you did something you shouldn't then any family member that was present had the authority to beat you. Grandparent, aunt or uncle, cousin, friend of the family.

The summer leading into his sophomore year of high school, Cliff worked a farm job to buy his school clothes. At night, he hung out with white friends, drinking and smoking pot. When school started, Cliff regained his starting position on the football team.

I was very productive on the field, in the classroom I wasn't. I had become the class clown, and in most of my classes I was doing just enough to get by. My English teacher was a friend of the family, but she was also a strict teacher. I was given a failing grade in English.

Cliff got kicked off the football team because of his grades. He played in the marching band and got his grades up enough by basketball season to play on the varsity team. For a short time, he dealt pot, with others, on a small scale, but quit, in part because of the attention it was drawing. He remembered:

My sophomore year in high school opened doors that it took me years to close. I started getting the attitude that I did not care what people thought.

For Cliff, growing up, racism was always close, the wild beauty of the woods and water undergirded by generations of brutality. Butterflies flutter near the grace of goodness not given. Just a few miles west on US 64 from Columbia, outside the town of Creswell, were the remains of Somerset Place, a plantation, or, more accurately, forced labor camp, where hundreds of enslaved Black workers had been whipped in the fields to enrich their white "masters" from 1785 until 1865. For Cliff's parents, the descendants of enslaved persons in the region, the history was real; the scars never healed, despite the history books Cliff was issued to read in school that painted slavery as a benevolent institution. Near the jail where he was held in Columbia on Stacey's case is a Confederate statue. It prominently features these words: "With appreciation for our faithful slaves."

Cliff knew better. A maternal great-great grandmother he knew as a boy was said to have been born into slavery around the time of the Civil War and freed with the war's end. His paternal great-great grandfather was an enslaved man who ran off to join the Union in the war.

Just over one hundred years later, when Cliff was in high school in the 1970s, the case of Joan Little in Beaufort County, catty-cornered to Cliff's home county, attracted worldwide attention. Little, a Black woman in her twenties, was being held on relatively minor charges in the jail in "Little Washington," the Beaufort County seat, when she was charged with first-degree murder in 1974 for fatally stabbing a white jailer whom she said made sexual advances toward her. Little won at trial.

Around the same time, two Black women in Cliff's Albemarle Sound region, Nial Cox Ramirez and Elaine Riddick, who had had been forcibly

Downtown Columbia. *John Railey.*

sterilized as teenagers by a State of North Carolina program that ultimately targeted Black women and girls of limited means, fought back as adults and sued the state, losing but making nationwide news.

After graduating from high school, Cliff attended Elizabeth City State University, a nearby historically Black university, playing in the school band and majoring in music. He found that major was not for him and dropped out of Elizabeth City State after two years. He enlisted in the army, served in Germany and returned to Columbia after he was discharged. His German wife came with him, and they had a daughter. Cliff worked blue-collar jobs, including driving delivery trucks for local construction companies.

In the year before his arrest, Cliff struggled. His wife left him, taking their toddler and going back to Germany. "Columbia was so different for her, and I should have realized that," Cliff would later say. In the six or seven months before his arrest, Cliff began doing crack cocaine with friends. It wasn't a long time, but it was a heartbreaking one.

Once, his father, trying to find Cliff to drive him to a job, found him in a crack house in Columbia where he had cashed his paycheck and spent it on crack. The incident brought tears to the eyes of Cliff's father. It broke Cliff's heart as well.

The New Jersey cocaine charge in the months before Cliff was charged with Stacey's murder had been part of that sad cycle. Cliff said he was headed for New York City to buy cocaine and was pulled over in his Nissan Sentra in Salem, New Jersey, just north of the Delaware River Bridge. He was pulled for "driving while Black," Cliff said. Officers found no coke in his car, he said, but did find enough residue to make a drug charge against him and confiscate his car. Ironically, he was busted in Stacey's home area, although they didn't know each other at the time.

In prison after being convicted in Stacey's murder, Cliff realized he'd been a crackhead. The addiction led him to the people who landed him in prison, he realized. His head was finally clear.

Cliff, negotiating his way through the mean politics that is prison life, began to work on his appeal. As he did so, he realized two truths about the criminal justice system that many laypeople never grasp: Prosecutors are not legally obligated to establish a motive for the conviction they are pursuing. Many convictions have been won without a motive, as was Cliff's. And while defendants are presumed innocent and are under no legal obligation to establish a theory another perpetrator may have acted on, juries, judges and prosecutors want that. The appeals process can demand it.

Cliff borrowed worn law books from other inmates, read exhaustively from them and started to write, remembering, as best he could, the nights and days leading up to his arrest and his meetings with investigators after. He set his pen to a yellow legal pad and started to write a motion for appropriate relief (MAR). He wrote neatly in print, all caps.

Cliff described arriving at the Green Dolphin on the night of Friday, February 2, and seeing his friends Stacey and Mike Brandon. The scene he laid out started innocently enough, just friends on a Friday night. "Once I got in the pub I saw a couple of friends, Mike Brandon and Elizabeth Stacey Stanton. When I entered the pub, Mike was playing pool and Stacey was on the other side of the game room, standing by the juke box," Cliff wrote.

Brandon with his good looking, long-haired brooding presence, fun until he got too drunk and got mean, wanting to fight. Stacey, blonde and beautiful but never stuck-up about it, standing like a dream by the record machine. Cliff had met Brandon a couple of years before, through coke, and soon met Stacey, whom Brandon had lived with until several weeks before the slaying.

Cliff wrote:

> I spoke to Mike and I waved at Stacey. I never spoke to Stacey while I was in the bar. The whole time I was there, I talked to Mike. He was the only person there besides Stacey that I was on a friendly basis with. I was also the only Black in the game room. I was there for about 30 to 45 minutes when Mike walked over to Stacey and said something. I could not hear what he said, but it upset Stacey and she left. I ask [sic] what that was all about and he told me that he wanted her to leave. He said he had broken up with her and he had started dating a young lady....He said Stacey was trying to make trouble for him and [his new girlfriend]. So I let it drop.

Cliff described a friendlier time with Brandon than Brandon had related to the investigators. "We started drinking beer. I would buy a round for both of us, and then he would buy a round," Cliff wrote.

Cliff wrote that he stayed in the bar "for an hour, maybe longer" before he left and started walking to the home of his Manteo friend Wayne Morris. Along the way, he wrote, Stacey called to him from where she was standing in the parking lot of her Ananias Dare Street apartment, taking to a man he did not know. "She asked me if I knew what was going on," Cliff wrote. "She was talking about her and Mike in the club....She was drunk and talking very loudly. Her words were slurred. Once we got to her apartment,

I asked her what was wrong. She told me that she had broken up with Mike, and that she wanted to see if she could straighten things out."

> *We drank some vodka. I think I may have had 1 or 2 mixed drinks. Stacey was down and depressed. She asked me if I would go back to the Green Dolphin and ask Mike to come and see her later. I didn't want to go at first, but she asked me again and I said I would. So I left and went back to the pub....Mike was still playing pool so I went to the bar and got a couple of beers. I gave him his beer and related what Stacey had asked me to tell him. He told me to tell her that he was not going to come by her place. I stayed in the pub and drank another beer.*

During that time, he wrote, a white man tried to start a fight with him, and Mike seemed to be "going along with this man and his friends. I was the only Black in the pub. I told Mike he was just like the rest of those guys and left. I went back to Stacey's apartment. When I arrived there was another guy there, not the same man who was with her in the parking lot. I had seen this guy before but did not know his name."

Cliff wrote that went to the kitchen and poured a glass of 7-Up. "I told Stacey what Mike had said and she acted disappointed." Later, he wrote, he went to the bathroom, urinated and washed his hands. "When I returned the guy who was there was getting ready to leave. I'm not sure if he went in the bathroom or not before he left. Once he left and Stacey came back in the living room, she sat on my lap."

> *She was hurt by what happen* [sic] *between her and Mike and she was drunk. We talked for a while and she wanted to get high. I told her I did not have anything and she gave me $35 to go and see if I could find some. So I left to see if I could find someone who had some cocaine.*

Cliff wrote that he couldn't find any crack, went back to Stacey's apartment and told her he would try again later. Stacey "had a mattress on the living room floor" and was watching TV.

> *I got on the floor beside her on the mattress. At first I was laying there watching TV. I'd had too much to drink, so while I layed there, I fell asleep. I don't know long I was sleep* [sic]*, but I remember Stacey nudging me with her foot. She said something like you are not Mike. She was not angry with me when she woke me up and I decided to go to my friend Wayne*

Morris's house to spend the night. I got up, put on my shoes, I called to Stacey and told her I would see [her] *later. I don't know exactly where she was, but she told me bye and when I left the apartment, Stacey Stanton was alive.*

That was in the predawn hours of Saturday, February 3. Two days later, Cliff wrote, after Sergeant Steve Bell of the Tyrrell County Sheriff's Office picked him up, he met the investigators from Manteo:

One of them introduced himself as Chief of Police Day. The other said he was SBI Agent Inscoe. They sat down and asked me if I was in Manteo over the weekend. I told them yes I was. They told me they were investigating a murder and ask [sic] *me if I mind* [sic] *talking to them. I told them I did not mind at the time. I ask* [sic] *them who was killed. They told me that Stacey Stanton was dead and asked me if I knew it. I told them no, this was the first I'd heard of it. They ask* [sic] *me if I was at Stacey's over the weekend. I told them yes. They ask* [sic] *me when. I told them it was on Friday night and I asked them when all this was suppose* [sic] *to have happened. They would not tell me.*

Cliff wrote that he told the investigators he was unsure about the exact time he saw Stacey. The investigators pressed, Cliff wrote, and he told them he didn't wear a watch. He never saw either officer take notes on what he said, he wrote. "At the end of the interview," he added, "Agent Inscoe told me that 'It looked real bad for me.' He ask [sic] me if anyone saw me that night. I told him I stayed with my friend that night. His name was Wayne Morris."

Cliff wrote that he volunteered to take a lie detector test.

Sergeant Bell came back in in the interview room, Cliff wrote, and Agent Inscoe told Bell that Cliff was wanted in New Jersey for the drug charge, and they were going to extradite him. Bell arrested him on the fugitive warrant, Cliff wrote, and took him into custody, locking him up in a cell.

The next day, February 5, Cliff wrote, SBI agent Thompson gave him the lie detector test in a room at the Tyrrell County Courthouse, asking him if he cut Stacey and if he was present when she was cut. Thompson told Cliff he failed the test. "I told him that something must be wrong and we should do it again," Cliff wrote. "He told me the only way I could take it again was if I change my answer's [sic] and say that I killed Stacey. I told him I did not kill Stacey and I would not say that I did!"

He wrote that he did not remember Thompson "ever testing the machine to see if it was operating correctly."

Over the next several days, Cliff wrote, the investigators continued to question him, and he continued to say he did not kill Stacey. On February 8, he wrote, SBI agents Tony Cummings and Leroy Allen told him they thought Stacey attacked Cliff with a knife and said "I shook my head 'yes.'" But he wrote that he asked them, "'What are you talking about?' and stood up and told them 'I am going back to my cell.'"

That night about eight o'clock, Cliff wrote, a Tyrrell County deputy "came up to the cell block and told me to…come with him. I ask [sic] did I have to go down stairs [sic] and he told me I had to. When I got down stairs [sic] I saw Agent Cummings and Agent Allen. Agent Inscoe told me I was going with them, he ask [sic] me did I know where I was going to, I told him no, he told me Manteo."

The Tyrrell deputy told him he had to go, Cliff wrote.

> So I was under the impression there was nothing I could do but go with them. While on the way to Manteo, I told Agent Inscoe I want to see my lawyer, and does he know that you are taking me to another county? Agent Inscoe did not answer my question. Agent Inscoe tried to initiate a conversation with me. I pretend that I was a sleep [sic]. Once we got to Manteo, Agent Inscoe, who was driving, drove to Stacey's apartment and asked me if I would get out of the car and show him the route I walked from Stacey's house. I refused. They rode around, trying to get me to tell them the route I walked to my friend's house. I kept quiet. Then they told me they wanted to talk to me some more. I thought they were going to take me to the jail and talk to me, but they took me to Airport Road, which is a dead-end road.

On the airport grounds, Cliff wrote, the county had "converted a building into a drug enforcement office."

> There was no one there, and I did not want to go. They told me they wanted to talk with me without being interrupted. I said, "I do not have anything I want to talk about and I want to go back to the jail!" They still took me to the drug enforcement office. When I think back, I am sure they had this planned, to get me away from my lawyer, and family. Once we arrive [sic] at the drug enforcement office, I told Agent Inscoe that I wanted to call my lawyer so I could let him know where I am. He did

not let me call. He said he would call. He said he would call but he did not do this in my presence.

He left the room and left me with Agent Allen and Agent Cummings. I did not have anything to say to these 2 agents because I did not trust these 2 and I was afraid because no one knew where I was....While I was alone with Agent Cummings and Agent Allen, they did the same thing they did the first time I saw them. They started telling me what they thought happened. They ask [sic] me about why I was going to New Jersey, was it about drugs? Then they told me that they thought I was real high off drugs and did not know what I was doing.

I would not say anything because I was scared. There was a rifle sitting beside me, and after about 30 minutes to an hour they left me alone in the office with the rifle.

(Cliff later told the author that he did say a few words, just telling the investigators that he had nothing more to add to what he'd said in the previous interviews. The rifle sat on the interview table the whole time they talked, he said, and for all he knew, it was loaded. He wondered if the gun was there to intimidate him and, possibly, when the investigators left the room, to lead him into a confrontation with law enforcement.)

The investigators let him make a call, Cliff wrote.

I called my father and I told him where I was. I told him they took me to Manteo and I did not want to go. After I hung the phone up, I walk [sic] slowly out of the office and there were at least 8 officers in the hall including the ones that brought me there. I was frightened for my life and I kept asking them to take me back to jail. If I remembered something else, I would tell them tomorrow. But I do not know anything about the murder. After about another 15 minutes they took me back to Columbia. I was afraid, they took me away from familiar surroundings and away from my attorney and started making accusations.

The next day, February 9, in Columbia, Cliff wrote, SBI agents Cummings and Allen told his initial lawyer, Charles Ogletree, that Cliff told the agents that Stacey had attacked him with a knife. With his father and lawyer present, Cliff wrote, "I told Agent Cummings, Agent Allen and Chief Day that I did not say that Stacey attacked me with a knife, and that Agent Cummings and Agent Allen know I did not tell them that. After that I was taken back to my cell."

Cliff wrote that his conviction "was obtained in violation of due process," citing federal and state law. He noted that the Tyrrell County Sheriff's Department lacked the power "to release custody of the defendant to SBI agents without prior judicial intervention, whereby a writ of habeas corpus would be issued to take possession of the body the defendant" and that the conviction was "obtained due to the ineffectiveness of trial counsel," among many other contentions.

Cliff finished his seventy-seven-page motion for appropriate relief in the spring of 1992 and mailed it to the Dare County clerk of court on April 23. The clerk's office received it and stamped it as "filed" the next day.

Meanwhile, some Manteo locals had never stopped talking about Spencer's case. One of those locals was Deputy Terri Williams, who'd been the first law-enforcement officer at Stacey's crime scene. Sometime after that, she returned, after a long day of work, to her home on Twyne Lane, a gravel road on the North End of Roanoke Island, and found Mike Brandon and a troubled, naked woman whom Williams had given shelter on a couch. Brandon hopped up with a wild look in his eyes at Williams. Brandon had always given Williams a bad feeling, so the southpaw moved her left hand to the Beretta 9mm on her hip holster. The nude woman by Brandon's side calmed him down. Williams told them both to get the hell out of her house. They grabbed their clothes and did so.

Across the country and North Carolina, inmates file hundreds of thousands of handwritten motions annually seeking relief. Many, if not most, of those motions get nowhere. The criminal justice system, at least in North Carolina, is a huge, creaking, patched-up ship manned by lawyers all too human, plagued by conditions ranging from overwork to just plain laziness. Many handwritten motions are meritless, packed with lies. A relative few are the real thing, injustice really crying out for justice. Many lawyers, joking about how every inmate claims he's innocent, never take the time to sort out these motions assigned to them by judges. Valid motions that have taken inmates hundreds of hours to write end up in dusty file cabinets with little action taken on them.

Cliff got lucky.

14

ENTER THE FIGHTERS

There are a lot of unanswered questions in this case.
—Edgar Barnes, appellate attorney for Cliff Spencer

In June 1992, superior court judge Steve Michael found reason for consideration on one of Cliff's arguments in his motion for appropriate relief (MAR): that his counsel, Romallus Murphy, was ineffective. He appointed Edgar Barnes of Manteo to represent Cliff on that count.

Barnes soon told the *Coastland Times* that "he had not made up his mind about whether Spencer got competent legal representation or not, but that he had communicated with Murphy and was going to meet with him." When the matter comes to a hearing, Barnes said, his client would have to prove that he did not have effective representation. "We've got every bit of the burden in this case," he said. "There are a lot of unanswered questions in this case." Barnes noted that he had seen no written, signed confession.

Barnes, in his early thirties, was just starting his law practice in Manteo. He remembered hearing his law partners coming back from court the day Cliff had pleaded no contest in January 1991, saying the state's evidence was flimsy. He also knew that taking on the case would be an uphill battle. He was a white man taking on an appeal from a Black man for killing a white woman in a predominantly white county. He had thoughts of one day winning election to a judgeship.

Barnes, of medium build, five feet, eight inches tall, with short brown hair and bright dark eyes, rolls through life like a middle-weight boxer, on the balls of his feet. He grew up working on his family's blueberry farm in the Sandhills region of southeastern North Carolina. He graduated from the University of North Carolina at Wilmington, then secured his law degree from the North Carolina Central School of Law in Durham, a historically Black college and university.

He has a fierce commitment to justice and doing what is right. He and his wife, Michele, would soon start their family, and he wanted to do what he could to make a better world for their children. He dove into the case as Murphy had never done, first interviewing Cliff in prison. Barnes told Cliff he was impressed with his MAR. Cliff told Barnes that he was innocent.

Barnes noted that Cliff, in all the SBI interviews, had never confessed or admitted any guilt. The more he talked to Cliff, the more Barnes realized that his client, in his initial talks with the investigators, had thought he was trying to help find the killer of Stacey. Only too late did Cliff realize the lawmen were not his friends. They had been circling him like water moccasins if Cliff had fallen into a nest of them in one of his home waters, snakes swimming silent, deadly and in the dark.

Back in Manteo, Barnes went into neighborhoods, moonlighting between the rest of his work, interviewing witnesses, first on his own and later with the help of a private investigator. Word spread quickly as Barnes worked on the little island, causing some potential witnesses to shut up and others to relay tips.

Barnes drove the six hours to Greensboro, North Carolina, in the state's central Piedmont, to meet Murphy. Barnes talked with him for several hours in Murphy's office about Cliff's case. With Murphy's consent, Barnes made copies of all the discovery materials the state had given Murphy.

Barnes's investigation of the case was handicapped by the court's mandate that he explore only Murphy's work, not the actual evidence. But

Edgar Barnes. *Drew C. Wilson.*

the mandate still gave Barnes room to work. Barnes sought to raise public awareness of the case, once writing to the then-popular Maury Povich TV show, encouraging its producers to do a segment on the case. He noted in the letter that Murphy had never interviewed potential witnesses that Cliff had told him about. Murphy had coerced and scared his client into pleading no contest to a crime he did not commit, Barnes wrote.

"I also believe that the murderer of this poor young girl is still among us and thinks he may have possibly committed the perfect crime," Barnes wrote.

Cliff, because of the way Murphy had treated him, was initially wary of Barnes. But Cliff came to trust him. Barnes had represented Mike Brandon in several unrelated cases in 1990, after Stacey was killed that year. Barnes said he never developed a rapport with Brandon. Now, in 1992, as he worked Cliff's motion for appropriate relief for ineffective counsel, Barnes said he heard a rumor that Brandon had confessed to killing Stacey. Barnes had his private investigator track that down and question Brandon. The investigator got nowhere.

As Cliff talked with Barnes, he realized for the first time that Brandon had implicated him, the day Stacey's body was found, as the potential killer. He had no idea Brandon had been working against him. Murphy had never told him that, if Murphy had even read that part of the discovery.

Cliff Spencer at a court appearance in Manteo. *Drew C. Wilson.*

—m—

THE SHOWDOWN CAME IN the spring of 1993 during a two-day hearing that started on April 20 in the downtown Manteo Courthouse. The matter was heard in the wood-paneled courtroom on the second floor, the same room where Cliff had entered his no-contest plea in January 1991.

Cliff thought about that as a bailiff led him into the courtroom and he sat down at the defense table by Barnes. They talked quietly as they waited for superior court judge Gary Trawick to begin the hearing. Barnes told his client they had a fighting chance at a new trial.

Judge Trawick called the court to order. Murphy was the first witness Barnes called. The big man took his seat in the witness chair. Barnes began questioning him, a moment he and his client had long awaited and prepared for. Cliff stared at Murphy, who did not return his glance.

Murphy was solemn, clearly not happy to have his work questioned. Barnes was serious and confident as he began walking Murphy through the case. Through questioning, he determined that Murphy had not received the discovery documents from the district attorney's office until shortly after November 28. Such materials, which prosecutors are required by law to share with defense attorneys, lay out the prosecution case. Murphy testified that prosecutors indicated the delay had to do with securing the military records of Cliff's assault convictions in Europe. But he was uncertain about how much he had pressed prosecutors for the discovery.

Two things were obvious to the lawyers who stopped by the courtroom to watch: Murphy had begun pushing his client toward entering a plea before he had studied the discovery, and Cliff had entered that plea just over a month after it had been received, a time frame that would not have given his lawyer time to study the hundreds of pages in the materials, including the multiple interviews investigators did with Cliff.

As Barnes continued his questioning, it was clear Murphy did little with the discovery.

In fact, his lack of familiarity with the case was stunning, as demonstrated by one of his responses to Barnes's questions about what Cliff had told him about his movements around the time of Stacey's slaying.

"He indicated to me that he talked to some people at the Green Lantern or whatever the name of the club is, talked to Mike Brandon and had some dialogue with several people there," Murphy testified. "I think he went to the home of the deceased and came to talk to Mike about something."

It was remarkable that Murphy didn't know the name of the Green Dolphin or what Cliff's "dialogue" with Mike Brandon and others was about. Nor could he recall the name of the friend at whose house Cliff had crashed during the time around Stacey's killing. Murphy acknowledged that he was uncertain about when and where he had talked to Cliff.

He had not interviewed any potential witnesses, he acknowledged. He had not interviewed any of the investigators, he testified, and he had not visited the crime scene. He acknowledged that he had shared some of the discovery materials with Cliff and that Cliff repeatedly told him he was not guilty and would not plead guilty to a murder he didn't commit.

Barnes questioned Murphy about concerns the lawyer had voiced to Cliff about being a Black man charged with killing a white woman in a southern town. Murphy said: "I think that in this country, the issue of Black and white is one that a lawyer ought to be conscious if you happen to have a client in that situation."

But in response to further questions from Barnes, Murphy's answers revealed he had done little research on how local racial demographics might have affected a trial for Cliff.

Barnes called SBI agent Kent Inscoe. Inscoe acknowledged that, on February 8, 1990, when he and SBI agent Tony Cummings had driven Spencer from the Tyrrell County jail to Dare County, they did not have a judicial order to do so. That order should have been required, especially since Cliff was being held only on the fugitive warrant from New Jersey and had yet to be charged in Stacey's slaying.

> *Barnes:* "*What was your purpose in taking him after dark, at 8 o'clock, out of Tyrrell County Jail and driving him to Dare County, into a different county?*"
>
> *Inscoe:* "*At the time, he had given us a statement of where his exact path was* [on the night Stacey was killed] *and that time we were looking for a weapon.*" *Cliff agreed to make the trip, Inscoe testified.*
>
> *Barnes asked:* "*You couldn't do that the next day, the morning?*"
>
> *Inscoe:* "*Probably could have, yes sir.*"

Inscoe also acknowledged that Cliff had spent some of the early morning hours of February 3, the day Stacey's body had been discovered, at the Manteo home of Wayne Morris, and that no bloodstains were found at that home.

—⁂—

Soon thereafter, Barnes called former Manteo police chief Steve Day. He testified that the original jurisdiction for the case was with his department.

Barnes asked Day: "Chief, what was the strongest information you found, pursuant to your investigation of the case, that you thought suggested that he [Cliff] was actually the guilty party?"

Day: "The, I will use the word, the 'inconsistency' of his statements."

Barnes asked: "Chief, during your investigation of this case and the convolution of documents and statements, is there a signed statement by Clifton Spencer that you are aware of? That he signed a statement that he allegedly made?"

Day: "Not that I can recall right this moment."

Barnes: "Chief, in your opinion as one of the chief investigating officers in this case, what physical evidence in this case suggested that Clifton Spencer was guilty?"

Day replied that the SBI "handled and controlled" the physical evidence, so he couldn't "answer with any authority."

—⁂—

Barnes called Cliff's father, Harry Spencer. He testified that Murphy had pushed Cliff and his family into entering a plea and that Murphy had not pursued potential witnesses that Harry had suggested to him. And he talked about his son's concerns with the investigators' interviews of him. "He had told me several times that he talked to the SBI and certain things that he said, and they would twist his statement around and they would say that he said something else. And he said, 'Dad, I didn't tell them that.' Of course, they would tell me certain things that he told them, and I would ask him about it. And he would say, 'No, Dad, I didn't tell them that.'"

The father said Murphy, in encouraging his son to take a plea, said that "they would rip him apart if he took the stand and he wouldn't stand a chance."

Barnes told the court he had no further questions. District attorney H.P. Williams aggressively began his cross-examination, asking Harry Spencer, "What is that you just said? I didn't hear you."

Spencer: "He [Murphy] told me that if Cliff took the stand they would tear him apart and that he wouldn't stand a chance…him being a Black man, he wouldn't stand a chance anyway."

Williams: "And that is because your son had kept telling different stories to police at different times?"

Spencer: "No, I don't think that's the reason he [Murphy] told me that."

Next, Barnes called his client's mother, Emma Spencer. In the midst of Murphy's push for a plea, she testified, he told me "about all the evidence that the SBI had and all the things they said Clifton said. And I told him, 'Clifton said he didn't make those statements.' Mr. Murphy told me that it didn't make no difference because one SBI agent would say that Cliff said it, and another would come up and verify it. He didn't stand a chance."

—⁓—

FINALLY, BARNES CALLED CLIFF to the stand. He talked about the pressure Murphy had put on him to enter a plea and testified that Murphy had never shared with him, in depth, the discovery documents, much less Stacey's autopsy report or the physical evidence, at all. He never folded and agreed to enter a plea until hours before he walked into the court that morning, he testified.

> Barnes: *Clifton, why would you enter any plea whatsoever in this case?*
>
> Spencer: *Mr. Murphy gave me—I felt that when Mr. Murphy told me there was no way in the world I could win, I believed him. He was there to defend me. I didn't know nothing about the law. And he told me that if I went in there, I couldn't win, nobody would believe me. I felt, I just, I couldn't do anything.*
>
> Barnes: *What, if anything, did Mr. Murphy tell you would happen to you if you did try this case?*
>
> Spencer: *That I would lose and that I would die.*

On cross-examination by district attorney Williams, Cliff acknowledged his convictions in Germany, while in the army, of assault.

—⁓—

IN HIS CLOSING ARGUMENT, Barnes said,

> *It appears your honor, that for six months* [from the time Murphy was retained in Cliff's case until Cliff gave up and agreed to enter a plea], *Mr. Murphy waited. And Judge, I will be trying cases,*

hopefully if I am lucky, for many more years. And I will probably have an allegation like this made against me; I'm not perfect and I don't expect Mr. Murphy to be perfect. But in this particular case, Judge, Clifton Spencer, if he had known, if he had had a chance, if his attorney had given him any hope and if he had known any facts about the case—which he didn't other than [saying] *"These are the statements they said you made.".... Judge, he* [Murphy] *should have made some independent investigation or talked to someone and tried to verify whether those statements were accurate or whether they were not.*

Judge Trawick noted to Barnes that Murphy had filed motions in the case shortly before Cliff entered his plea. Barnes responded that, in recommending that his client take a plea, Murphy should have investigated the case just as hard as if he was going to trial.

That is recommended practice in death penalty cases.

Barnes said:

You just can't sit back and do nothing, just because—in this case Mr. Murphy didn't anticipate, he never knew, that there was going to be a plea....And [he] *told you he had not talked to anybody. He had not done any investigation at all about this case up to that point. How in the world would* [Cliff] *have known anything about his case? The fact is that Murphy could have done something, Judge, I mean, he could have done something....*

And Judge, I am asking you to consider that due to the ineffectiveness of counsel in not informing his client of relevant facts in this case and of his options that his plea was not an informed, voluntary and intelligent plea in this case.

In his close, district attorney Williams stood up for Murphy, saying,

I don't think you could say that he did nothing....He traveled on several occasions and interviewed the defendant, met with his family, had filed the motions and obtained the discovery....I think it was clear that [Cliff] *was insisting on going to trial. And then it was his own voluntary decision to change his mind. There has been no showing of counsel's errors....There has been no showing that confidence in the administration of justice has been undermined in any way.*

Judge Trawick denied Cliff's motion, writing, "The plea was entered into voluntarily," effectively ruling that the defense counsel was effective.

Before bailiffs led Cliff out of the courtroom, Barnes told his client he would keep fighting for him. Cliff just nodded his head.

In a July 2023 interview with the author, Trawick said he would probably make the same ruling today. Before taking the bench, he said, he had, as a defense attorney, handled numerous murder cases, including some death-penalty ones. In ruling on the MAR, he said, he felt bound by Judge Herbert Small's January 1991 acceptance of Cliff's no contest plea. "One superior court judge doesn't overrule another," he said.

Asked if that was not the point of a MAR, to allow for such action if justified, Trawick said it was not justified in Spencer's case. Trawick, however, was unable to cite any actions Murphy had taken on Cliff's case. Perhaps the investigators erred on the case, he suggested, or perhaps district attorney Williams had erred in initially going for the death penalty, instead of a lesser charge.

In retirement in 2022, Trawick published a memoir on race relations in the South. "Judge Trawick shares how he came to grips with misplaced hate, endemic racism and toxic culture," according to the book's website.

—m—

IN APRIL 1994, MIKE Brandon was convicted of several counts of larceny and breaking and entering in Dare County and sentenced to ten years in prison. His marriage to Patty Rowe had ended. She would later say that was because of the beatings he gave her, culminating in one that left her with a head wound so bad her skull was exposed.

—m—

BARNES APPEALED TRAWICK'S DECISION to the North Carolina Court of Appeals. The higher court denied the appeal in June 1994.

After that denial, Barnes told the *Coastland Times*, "The most significant thing that has influenced me is the people in the court system and the community have told me you need to help this man." He noted that "there seemed to be a rush to find a suspect and conclude the case."

Barnes's private investigator, Asher Vandenburg, gave Cliff a new polygraph test, asking him whether he participated in Stacey's slaying. "After a careful and detailed analysis of the polygraph charts…I have determined that Mr. Spencer is not guilty of causing the death of Stacey Stanton," Vandenburg, a state-certified polygraph examiner, wrote, according to the *Virginian-Pilot* newspaper.

In 1995, Barnes wrote a letter to Frank Parrish, who'd beaten Parrish's boss, H.P. Williams, to win election as district attorney in 1994. "I sincerely and personally believe Clifton Spencer to be innocent and will continue to fight to see that he receives due justice,'" Barnes wrote. "I ask you to consider reopening this case. Or at least let me have access to all the police officers' investigation files in order that I might be satisfied that justice has been served."

District Attorney Frank Parrish, who succeeded H.P. Williams. *Kim Parrish.*

Parrish told Lane DeGregory of the *Virginian-Pilot* that he would look into the evidence, review internal and police files and, eventually, meet with investigators. "I'm not saying I will reopen this case," he said. "But I'm very willing to look into it. My only concern—always and for every case—is that justice be done."

North Carolina governor Jim Hunt appointed Barnes to a new district court judgeship in Dare County. Drew Wilson of the *Virginian-Pilot* snapped a fine shot of Barnes, looking serious in his new black robe, his pretty wife, Michele, by his side, holding their blond toddler, Graham. In an interview with the *Virginian-Pilot* newspaper in July 1995, as he took the bench, Barnes emphasized his continued belief that Cliff was innocent.

"I'm going to swear to uphold justice," Barnes told DeGregory. "And I will do that for Clifton Spencer, I'm not going to forget about him. I'm going to do as much as I can for him without violating legal ethics. I'm not convinced justice has been done in this case."

He talked about the evidence. "The police photographs show Caucasian hair all over Stacey's right chest wall," Barnes said. "Clifton Spencer has an alibi between 4 and 5 a.m. that day from his friend, Wayne Morris. He has an alibi from 5 a.m. that morning from the people who drove him back to Columbia."

Top: Judge Edgar Barnes; his wife, Michele; and their child, Graham, at his swearing in as a District Court judge in 1995. *Drew C. Wilson.*

Bottom: Cliff Spencer during a prison interview in the summer of 1995. *Drew C. Wilson.*

DeGregory, who would later win a Pulitzer Prize for feature writing unrelated to Cliff's case, interviewed Cliff at the Gates Correctional Center:

> *He sleeps on the bottom bunk in a cinderblock prison dormitory he shares with 35 other inmates. With no air conditioning—and only two small windows that open—nights get so unbearably hot that no one can sleep, Spencer said in a telephone interview Thursday.*
>
> *"That's when I come close to giving up," said the 36-year-old Army veteran, who previously was convicted of drug possession and assault on a female.*
>
> *"It's 100 degrees or more and no one even remembers I'm here. Now that Edgar is a judge, I won't have any outside help," Spencer said. "I just want someone to look at my whole case. I want a judge or jury to see all the evidence. Ultimately, I'd just like to have a trial.*
>
> *"I've lost my freedom for something I didn't do."*

DeGregory's colleague, photographer Drew Wilson, shot photos in which Cliff is pensive and thoughtful, mournful intelligence in his eyes. Wilson remembered later that Spencer "seemed like a normal guy in a bad predicament who was doing what he could to tell his story. He didn't seem openly bitter or angry. He may have had that under the surface."

Lieutenant Colonel Jasper Williams stood by their work. "We spent months investigating that case. And the SBI has all of the evidence and reports now," he told the *Pilot*. "If I had any doubts at all about having the right man, I'd still be pursuing this case. As it stands, this case has been closed for four years."

Letitia Echols of the Raleigh-based nonprofit North Carolina Prisoner Legal Services, who had been representing Spencer since 1994, told the *Pilot*: "There is a possibility that we could file a federal appeal. But we haven't done so yet. I've held onto this case because I think there's something there. I need to interview some witnesses and some of the original investigators. And I plan to come to Dare County soon. His Greensboro attorney didn't really even go through the evidence. We're looking into the case now. I think there is something there. I'm just trying to nail it down."

"Even if a federal level appeal is successful, Spencer wouldn't walk," Echols told the *Pilot*. "He would just get a trial."

DeGregory's hard-hitting story ran on the front page of the *Pilot* on July 4, 1995.

Spencer reacts during the prison interview. *Drew C. Wilson.*

One of the readers was Bobbie McGuinness. She was the local woman who had told the investigators of the troubles between Mike Brandon and Stacey at the Green Dolphin pub hours before Stacey was killed. She'd long been bothered by the case. Brandon had worked for her as a painter, and she found him to be "very volatile on occasion." She would never forget the anger on his face that night at the Green Dolphin. It was like he was in a rage, she said, like he was being forced into a situation.

She'd kept her silence, intimidated by the threat that Mike Brandon's sister, Tina, had told her about not implicating Brandon. But now, McGuinness was motivated by the truth.

She tracked down Cliff at the latest prison to which he'd been transferred, Caswell Correctional Center in the central part of North Carolina, called him and left a phone message with prison officials. Cliff was unable to return the call. McGuinness contacted Barnes and told him about the interview she had given investigators. District attorney Williams had never turned over that interview to Murphy or Barnes, although it was potentially exculpatory, favorable to the defense, and should have been part of the normal discovery process. Barnes reported McGuinness's contact info to Echols, the attorney with North Carolina Prisoner Legal Services.

Spencer makes his case in the prison interview. *Drew C. Wilson.*

Echols, like Barnes, was a fighter. One of her first actions for Cliff was to file a motion that the evidence in his case be preserved. North Carolina law enforcement often failed to preserve evidence as cases aged.

And in 1997, she brought a new motion for appropriate relief, on the basis of the McGuinness interview, in Dare County Superior Court. The motion was denied. Echols appealed to the North Carolina Court of Appeals, which ordered the superior court to hold a hearing on the matter. The issues were whether the state had failed to disclose exculpatory evidence prior to Cliff's plea and, if so, whether the defendant's plea was voluntary as a result.

—⚭—

MEANWHILE, IN 1997, PATTY Rowe Brandon filed for divorce from Mike Brandon, who was imprisoned. In the filing in Dare County Superior Court, she said she and Brandon had been separated since October 1997. The separation was caused by "acts of domestic violence" by Mike Brandon, according to the filing. Their child had "witnessed at least some of these acts," according to the filing, and the Dare County Department of Social Services "performed an investigation and recommended therapy for the minor child, and that the child have no contact with the defendant [Mike Brandon]."

Spencer during the prison interview. *Drew C. Wilson.*

Patty Brandon complied with that, the filing said. The child was diagnosed with post-traumatic stress disorder, and "the cause of this trauma appears to have been the incidence of domestic violence in the child's household," the filing said, but now the child "appears to be doing well in school and appears to have a good relationship with [Patty Brandon]."

Mike Brandon, from prison, shot back his response, seeking to retain custody of their son. He sought legal representation for his fight, noting that he had just $6.97 in his prison canteen.

The divorce was granted, with Patty Brandon receiving sole custody of their child.

15

THE NEW APPEAL

The threat and "other things that happened in the community led me to move out of this area because I felt very uncomfortable here."
—Bobbi McGuiness at an appeal hearing in Manteo, January 1998

T he initial hearing on Cliff's second motion for appropriate relief was held on January 20, 1998, at the Manteo Courthouse. Assistant district attorneys Robert Trivette and Amber Davis represented the state. Superior court judge Richard Parker presided.

Defense attorney Letitia Echols began by calling Bobbi McGuinness to the stand. She testified about what she had told the investigators. And she added a bombshell: while at the Green Dolphin, she overheard Patty Rowe, Mike's girlfriend, saying that "if Stacey didn't leave Mike alone, she would kill her." The threat and "other things that happened in the community led me to move out of this area because I felt very uncomfortable here," she testified.

—⁂—

ECHOLS CALLED EDGAR BARNES to the witness stand. Barnes, who had represented Cliff on his first MAR and was now a district court judge, testified that the investigators' interview with Bobbi McGuinness was not in the discovery materials that he had secured from Romallus Murphy, the materials that Murphy had been given by the state. And the state had never given him the McGuinness interview to him as he worked on the MAR.

> *Echols: In your legal opinion, do you believe that testimony would have produced exculpatory evidence on Cliff's behalf?*
> *Barnes: Yes ma'am, I do.*
> *Echols: Thank you. No further questions.*

Assistant district attorney Trivette went at Judge Barnes on cross-examination but was unable to disprove Barnes's testimony that the state had not provided to the defense the interview.

Judge Parker asked Echols if she had other witnesses to call. The defendant, she said, but his testimony would take a while. Judge Parker continued the hearing until March 30, 1998.

—⁂—

ECHOLS BEGAN THE MARCH 30 hearing on a strong note, stating that, the month before, assistant district attorney Trivette had sent her office the SBI transcription of its interview with McGuinness.

Echols called Cliff to the witness stand. He had been transferred to the Currituck County Detention Center on the mainland, just across the Currituck Sound from that county's Outer Banks side. In response to questions from Echols, he testified that he knew Mike Brandon and Stacey had argued at the Green Dolphin in the hours before Stacey's body was found. "Well, when I first initially walked in the door, I could sense the tension in between the two of them and he said something to her, and she ran out so I knew they had an argument." He had heard testimony at the first part of the hearing in January, he said, and had been unaware of all the details to which McGuinness testified.

Echols asked Cliff if he knew what happened to the blood, hair and other samples the SBI had taken from him in the early stages of case. He said he did not. She showed her client the document that said no "Negroid" hairs were found (on Stacey's body). Cliff testified that he did not know of that finding when he entered his plea.

> *Echols: If you had known the full extent of the argument between Patty and Stacey and Mike and Stacey at the time you decided to enter that plea of no contest, would you have entered that plea of no contest?*
> *Cliff: No ma'am.*
> *Echols: I have no further questions at this time.*

On cross-examination, assistant district attorney Trivette hammered away at Cliff on the statements he had allegedly given investigators. On one point, Cliff was especially firm: he never told investigators that Stacey came at him with a knife and had told them that after an interview in which the investigators quoted him on that.

Cliff acknowledged that Murphy may have had many of the SBI reports before he entered his plea but emphasized that he had never seen the reports.

—⁂—

ECHOLS CALLED JUDGE BARNES to the stand. He testified that the first time he saw the McGuinness statement was February 19, when Echols had faxed it to him, after she had received it from the state. Echols asked him if the statement would have made a difference at the hearing on his motion for appropriate relief.

> Barnes: *All these factors, if I would have known them, I would have argued that there was another person who had a much stronger motive and just as much opportunity in this case to have committed this crime than Clifton Spencer.*
>
> Echols: *With this report, would this report have affected your investigation in any way?*
>
> Barnes: *I did an extensive investigation in this case after I was appointed. And I say "extensive" based on my inexperience as an investigator. I talked to many, many witnesses and I ran into a lot of dead-ends, and I talked to a lot of people who knew more rumor than they did fact.*

Barnes testified that he "would most definitely" have benefited from talking to McGuinness in the investigation and calling her as a witness at the original MAR hearing. "And I found that during my investigation as an amateur that one small lead usually leads to many leads as far as gathering evidence."

—⁂—

ECHOLS CALLED SBI AGENT Kent Inscoe, first concentrating on the statement the investigators had taken from McGuinness on February 6 at the sheriff's office in Manteo. But he testified that it wasn't until March

15, more than a month after the interview, that he dictated his notes from the interview for transcription.

Later, assistant district attorney Trivette called Inscoe back to the stand and asked him about Mike Brandon being a suspect in the case:

> *Inscoe: Mike Brandon was probably the first focus we had....And he was interviewed. He gave a statement. We then in turn interviewed people that had been with him or were his alibis of where he had been. We spoke with them. He was interviewed on more than one occasion. And we went from there.*
> *Trivette: Okay. All right. So, he had alibi witnesses during the time this murder occurred?*
> *Inscoe: Yes he did.*

Another witness Echols called, Cathy Rogers, who'd worked at the Green Dolphin, testified that locals were afraid of Mike Brandon because "he is just very reckless. He has been in and out of jail for most of his life and he is just very reckless." Brandon had a history of abusing women, she testified. Her statement to the SBI, while different from her testimony, had not been provided to the defense.

> *Echols: Are there people you know who have been abused?"*
> *Rogers: I do know he abused Patty and I did know of him abusing Stacey, slapping her around.*
> *Echols: When he abused Patty, what was the form of abuse?"*
> *Rogers: He has punched her, he has hit her, he's—they have had a lot of arguments. One time when I was working, he threw his six-pack of beer through the window at her at the pool table and since that day they have both been barred.*

—⁂—

IN HIS CLOSING ARGUMENT, Trivette argued that McGuinness's statement was not exculpatory:

> *If* [district attorney] *H.P. Williams was going to sit down, read this, decide whether this was exculpatory, your honor, I can't imagine any of us would have looked at this and said, "Oh gosh, we've got to give them this." If this is exculpatory, then everything is exculpatory.*

But Echols argued that the statements of Bobbi McGuinness and, for that matter, those of Cathy Rogers, were exculpatory.

"The bottom line is, what would Clifton Spencer have done if he had the advantage of those statements?" she asked. "Would he still have pled no contest? Would he have given up on his defense? Would he have decided to spend the rest of his life in prison to avoid a death penalty for something he is sure he did not do?

"There was evidence withheld. The evidence was exculpatory and without this information he could not have reasonably decided what to do with this case."

The judge entered his decision a few weeks later. He wrote that the statements of Bobbi McGuinness and Cathy Rogers were not exculpatory, and neither would have led "or caused the defendant to change his plea in the case."

Judge Parker's decision was devastating. Barnes's original MAR hearing and Echols' follow-up were strong, the closest Cliff had come to a trial, and the evidence of injustice was glaring. Judge Parker would tell the author in 2023 that, because of the high number of hearings he presided over during his career, he did not remember Cliff's second MAR hearing.

Echols did score one victory: her motion to preserve the evidence in Cliff's case was granted.

—⁘—

IN DECEMBER 2002, CLIFF'S sister Karen emailed the North Carolina Center on Actual Innocence in Durham, seeking help with her brother's case. Attorney Chris Mumma serves as its executive director. Her agency receives hundreds of such letters annually. Mumma, quietly charismatic, blonde and blue-eyed, makes it a point to read each one.

The wrongly imprisoned often visit her in dreams. She awakens in the middle of the night, gets out of bed and explores new strategies to help them. "I can't think of anything worse than being locked in a cell for something I didn't do," Mumma told the author. She's friendly but direct and knows instinctively when to pour on the charm or play tough.

She forgoes a salary at the innocence center so that the organization can hire more workers. She's a wealthy Republican who gave up a corporate career and does much of her own investigating, often in rough neighborhoods. She says freeing the innocent and prosecuting the guilty

Defense attorney Chris Mumma took on Spencer's case in the early 2000s. *Courtesy Chris Mumma.*

should be something everybody supports. This is as much about public safety as it is freeing the innocent.

But for too long in North Carolina, Democrats and Republicans alike, from the courthouse to the statehouse, shied away from confronting myriad problems in North Carolina's criminal justice system, such as shoddy and irresponsible work by investigators, forensic scientists, prosecutors and defense attorneys.

Mumma was climbing the ladder at Nortel, a telecommunications and data networking company, and starting a family when she decided to become a corporate lawyer. She didn't home in on criminal law until her third year in law school at the University of North Carolina in Chapel Hill. Three things opened her eyes to the need for reform: representing indigent clients for class credit, a paper she wrote about being a juror in a murder trial and working, after graduation, as a North Carolina Supreme Court clerk for then-chief justice I. Beverly Lake Jr. It was there that she saw firsthand how the question of someone's innocence was off the table for review after the jury returned a verdict or someone took a plea offer. Several cases she worked on concerned her, and she became convinced there were more than just a few innocent people serving time in North Carolina prisons.

After her clerkship, she went to work for the newly formed North Carolina Center on Actual Innocence, an umbrella organization for innocence projects at North Carolina law schools where students study cases to determine the merits of innocence claims and the possibilities for relief. She continued her close relationship with Chief Justice Lake, and they went on to work with others to champion criminal justice reform in North Carolina, including the establishment of the first state-funded innocence claims review agency, the North Carolina Innocence Inquiry Commission.

While working at the Center on Actual Innocence, Mumma freed some defendants wrongly convicted. And she became convinced there are more innocent people in our prisons, being punished for crimes others committed.

She received and carefully considered the email from Cliff's sister, which led to her obtaining and studying documents on his case. She visited Cliff in prison and came to believe in the merits in his claims.

Mumma had a special feel for the case. Like Stacey was, Mumma is from New Jersey, albeit North Jersey and not Stacey's South Jersey.

Mumma corresponded with Judge Edgar Barnes. And she sought records from district attorney Frank Parrish.

Mumma developed a solid working relationship with Parrish. A graduate of the University of North Carolina at Chapel Hill and Campbell University Law School, he had worked for his predecessor, district attorney H.P. Williams as an assistant district attorney from 1979 through 1993. He had met with investigators on Stacey's case before Cliff was charged, telling investigators they needed more evidence for that charge. Ultimately, Williams overrode him. Parrish studied the file as he corresponded with Mumma, who pointed out to him the many problems in the case.

Mumma liked Parrish. And she had a lawyer's sense of his character, what made him tick and how to harness that to help her client. Parrish was a committed Episcopalian who tried to live out his faith, including through a commitment to social justice and criminal justice.

16

LETTERS FROM CLIFF

If you would check the lab reports from when they tested the hair [found on Stacey's body] *in the first place, you will see that they stopped testing after there was no Negroid hair found.*
—*Cliff Spencer in a November 11, 2003 letter to attorney Chris Mumma*

Throughout the early 2000s, Cliff wrote his new lawyer, Chris Mumma, a series of letters. Mumma would occasionally write Cliff, but her communication with him was mainly through frequent visits and phone calls. In the letters, Cliff's street smarts and increasing knowledge of the legal system shine through. He was guarded at first. Then, he slowly began to trust his new lawyer and even form a friendship with her. He eventually dropped his guard and became candid with Mumma about his wild life, which led him to being charged in Stacey's slaying, while always maintaining his innocence. He freely wrote about his failings as a husband and father and how he hoped to turn his life around if he could ever get out of prison.

In a letter dated November 5, 2003, Cliff wrote to Mumma, worried about his case:

> *The reason for this letter is to thank you and your office for looking into my case. Even though what you shared with me was positive, I have a hard time believing in a positive outcome. Over the years I have heard positive reports just to have things fall apart. I know that you never guaranteed*

results, and it doesn't have to do with your office.…If [DA] *Parrish does write a letter of recommendation of parole in my case it couldn't hurt. I don't know if it would be a deciding factor unless it's a sincere effort…*
Sincerely,
Clifton

In a follow-up letter to Mumma dated November 11, 2003, Cliff pointed out the key injustice.

I don't know if this is an issue anymore, but if you would check the lab reports from when they tested the hair [found on Stacey's body] *in the first place, you will see that they stopped testing after there was no Negroid hair found.*

The reason why I am bringing this up is that I have thrown all of these years into thinking that something like that should have been completely tested to other suspects. By them stopping the tests after they found that my hair did not match the hair they got makes me think that they wanted it to be ME. Ms. Mumma, I truly want to be wrong about this, but if you can find a reasonable explanation with what you can find in the discovery evidence, please help me understand.

I don't want to sound like a broken record, so I'll bring this letter to an end…thank you for the prayers.
Sincerely,
Clifton

Mumma let Cliff know she was well aware of that glaring lab finding.

Cliff began a March 10, 2004 letter with "Hi Chris" instead of the "Dear Ms. Mumma" he had been starting with, signifying his growing comfort with his lawyer. He worried about a recent bout of hepatitis and wrote that he wanted to get out of prison while he was still able to enjoy his daughter. He was brutally honest about what kind of father and husband he had been.

I am a "forgotten" person in the system if it had not been for YOU and the project of actual innocence; me and other men and women like me would never have a chance to be treated fairly. I've lost my family, my freedom even though I was a lousy husband and father. I lost the chance to try and right the wrongs in my marriage, and be a father. Chris, I do want the chance to at least try and explain to my daughter why I was never there.

In a March 16 letter to Mumma, Cliff worried more about his case and his life.

> *I'm sorry, it has been a long time since I've relived those things I have questioned for so many years. Chris, it is a lot easier for me to think there was a "simple" mistake instead of believing that any of this was intentional. How I feel is hard to explain. I try not to "feel." I know that the years I've lost cannot be replaced and I try not to say…"what if." If I was never locked up would I have still been a father and husband? Would I have savings for my daughter's future?*
> *Sincerely,*
> *Cliff*

In a letter to Mumma dated March 22, Cliff thanked her for a recent visit, and worried that district attorney Parrish would not come through on his letter recommending Cliff for parole.

> *I don't believe that Mr. Parrish is going to write the letter and I don't think he will cooperate at all….They are not going to do anything to make them look like they made an* [error]*.…Chris, this thing is more like a game to them and I am the piece they are toying with.…I've had two different appropriate relief hearings which were jokes and, to be honest with you, I don't think a defendant can ever get a fair ruling in an appropriate relief hearing. So we are back to the hair evidence. If it is testable, we need to test it. I don't even trust the lab that tested it, I just can't shake the feeling that something else will come up missing.*
>
> *I really did not talk much about strategy with you because the only thing we can do you are doing…They are determined to keep me here in prison. I am willing to do whatever you need me to do to expose the investigation of my case.…*
>
> *Chris, I have so much on my mind and although I was listening to you* [when you were here on a recent visit] *in some ways I am dead. I will never forget what happened and it affected how I communicate with others. I am not as trusting as I once was. I do believe that our justice system can work but it doesn't.*
>
> *Edgar Barnes gave me hope when he took my case and what he told me was the truth and I believed that the system would work for me. Letitia Echols gave me hope when she took over my case and what she said was the truth and I still believed the system would work for me. You have given*

*me hope when you took over my case and what you have told me I believe
because it is the truth. But I know now that the system is not set up to be
fair and work....*

*So don't ever be hesitant to tell me bad news because the worst news
that was reported happened in February 1990 when they said I was the
person that killed Stacey....Chris, I'm not bitter anymore because I couldn't
continue to live with that, I do want my freedom. I pray it will be soon. I
know there is no way to accelerate the progress but I am always "hopeful"
that I will be home soon.*

—⁄⁄⁄—

But on March 24, 2004, district attorney Parrish wrote a surprising letter
to the North Carolina parole commission arguing for Spencer's release:

*My familiarity with this case persuades me to the conclusion that it would
have been extraordinarily difficult to convince twelve jurors beyond a
reasonable doubt of Mr. Spencer's guilt because of the quality and quantity
of evidence available to the state was not particularly strong.*

*I understand that Mr. Spencer has sedulously complied with inmate
rules and regulations and has received no infractions in the last ten years.*

*For the foregoing reasons, I cannot in good conscience and do not oppose
parole for Mr. Spencer. I believe that his parole now would be consistent
with the proper administration of justice.*

The letter was a masterpiece of diplomacy, a subtle plea for justice.
Without attacking his predecessor as district attorney, Parrish made clear
that the case had serious problems and Spencer should be released. District
attorneys rarely write such letters.

The parole commission was not immediately persuaded. They denied
Spencer's parole.

Cliff wrote his teenage daughter, Dominique, in Germany about the
decision. She wrote him back.

Hi Papa.

*How are you doing? I'm doing okay! I was a little bit shocked when
I read your last letter. That's why it took me so long to answer your
letter. Sorry, but I didn't know how to handle this situation! But it's still
not a reason to stop writing or calling you. I read the articles from the*

newspaper, I didn't understand everything, but I think it in some parts it's better like this.

I'm so mad at the court in America.

I believe in you that you didn't do it!!!

I'm sad about what happened…

Love,

Dominique

—⚏—

MUMMA KEPT WORKING. In an April 21, 2004 letter to Cliff, Mumma tackled the bad news from the parole commission:

Although you said you weren't surprised by the decision of the parole commission, I was disappointed and a little surprised. Everyone I had spoken to felt the letter from the district attorney would be compelling.

She wrote that she had visited Chocowinity in northeastern North Carolina, where Mike Brandon was living. She did not find him at home, she wrote. She wrote that she had driven to Manteo and viewed Edgar Barnes's files, as well as court file photos from the crime scene. "It is completely obvious from the photographs that the hair scattered on Stacey's neck and chest is not from a Black man," she wrote.

Mumma was working on getting DNA testing on the hairs to compare them with the DNA of Cliff, Mike Brandon and Patty Rowe. DNA testing had been in its infancy when Cliff was coerced into his no contest plea in 1991.

—⚏—

IN AN AUGUST 23, 2004 letter to Mumma, Cliff wrote about his transformation in prison.

I was taught a harsh lesson during the investigative stage of this case and it has stuck with me over the years. When this all happened, I thought that God was giving me a "wake up" call to straighten my life out. I was so sure that they would find out that I had nothing to do with this. After I was put in prison I went through a stage where I felt I longer existed….So at this point I was not very trusting. I still feel that the SBI played "fill in the blank" when it came time to finding a suspect and I was tagged "it." So am I angry? Yes I am angry....

I doubt if I can ever fully explain the effect this whole thing has had on me, but I refuse to continue to let my situation control me.

Mumma scored some victories. In the summer of 2004, Joni Newman, who had in 1990 given investigators an alibi for Mike Brandon in the predawn hours of Stacey's killing on February 3, 1990, told Mumma that Brandon had a violent argument at her home with his new girlfriend and left Newman's house. He called back about 7:30 a.m., Newman said, asking to use Newman's truck. She said she believed Brandon killed Stacey and could no longer be his alibi.

Mumma also reached out to Stacey's relatives in New Jersey. They agreed with her with that Spencer was not the killer.

— ∞ —

IN AN OCTOBER 21, 2004 letter to Mumma, Cliff expressed worries about not hearing for a month from his daughter in Germany.

You know, one of the hardest things to do is explain what happened to someone when you don't fully understand it yourself. I really don't know how to explain what happened to me, and there is a good possibility I will never know the reason the state felt I would be the best candidate for a life sentence with everything available to them as far as physical evidence. I don't know if this is a case of malicious prosecution, but it comes to mind when I think about what happened. I don't allow myself to think too much about why because it hurts.

In a letter to Mumma dated January 12, 2005, Cliff addressed what happened when he was in Stacey's apartment:

Chris, the truth is I do not remember the sequence that everything happened [in] the night Stacey was killed, I shouldn't have said I never laid on the mattress. At one point I fell asleep and Stacey was the one who woke me up. I would like to go over all the statements. I will tell you about my past. Chris, I will not defend anything that I did in the past, I was not a nice guy....For reasons that I can't explain I have not thought a lot about the details of that night, and it has helped me adjust to being in prison.

—⚏—

IN A LETTER TO Mumma dated March 7, 2005, from the Gates County prison, Cliff enclosed a letter his daughter, Dominique, had written from Germany:

> *Hi Pappa,*
> *How are you doing? Mama and I are doing fine!*
> *Your lawyer called me two days ago.*
> *She explained to me your situation....*
> *I hope that everything is going good. She has got a very nice voice. We didn't*
> *talk that long....I hope everything is going to be all right.*
> *Love you, Dominique*
> *PS: Tell everybody I said hi*

—⚏—

IN AN AUGUST 17, 2005 letter to Mumma, Cliff wrote about receiving a pass to see his mother. His father picked him up at the Gates County prison and drove him to Columbia.

> *Chris, I cannot explain the feeling seeing my mother after five years and to*
> *be with her on her 70th birthday. She has been there for me the entire time I*
> *have been in this prison and I want to be able to help her. She has sacrificed*
> *all these years to help me. Now I want to give back to her.*

—⚏—

ALTHOUGH DISTRICT ATTORNEY PARRISH had been exemplary in writing the letter supporting parole for Cliff, he made it clear that little else could be done unless Mumma could prove who actually killed Stacey. That was frustrating as hell. The state should have found the real killer to start with. But Parrish did have a point, because of the way the flawed legal system had played out in the case in the previous judicial decisions.

Mumma was used to such high odds. She persuaded Parrish to run DNA tests on Mike Brandon, who was out of prison on the burglary convictions, and Patty Rowe. That testing did not conclusively clear Cliff nor implicate Brandon. She then pushed for DNA testing on the bloodstained green washcloth found in the parking lot of Stacey's apartment.

Cliff, at the Gates Correctional Center, found hope in the testing. "I feel very hopeful that we're going to get a break in this thing, and things will go my way for a change," he told a reporter.

The tests showed the DNA "came from someone other than Spencer," the *News & Observer* of Raleigh reported in August 2005, but there was no indication of who that "other" might be.

In a story in the Raleigh newspaper later that summer, Cliff made his case. The reporter retold the story about the statement that state's thin case had hinged on:

> *When an investigator asked Spencer whether Stanton provoked him with a box cutter, Spencer leaned forward in his chair, put his head down and nodded "yes" two or three times according to a detective's interview notes. But he now says police misunderstood. "I got tired of answering them," Spencer said, "I sighed and put my head down. They took that as a yes."*

The reporter clearly understood how weak the case was:

> *His [Cliff's] fingerprints were the only physical evidence linking him to the crime scene. Hair found in Stanton's hands and mouth came from someone else. There was no blood on Spencer's clothes or in the living room of the friend he visited later.*

The most intriguing quote was from the district attorney who put Cliff away:

> *"There were some serious questions about whether it could have been another individual," said H.P. Williams Jr., the district attorney who prosecuted Spencer and who now practices law in Elizabeth City. "I think the compelling evidence against Spencer was his inability to tell the truth during interviews. That doesn't mean he did it."*

Amazing. Williams's comment was not based on the new evidence but, apparently, on his view of the case in 1990. With doubts like that, why had he prosecuted Cliff? Why had he not reopened the case?

The reporter also recounted Joni Newman's recantation of her alibi for Mike Brandon.

> *A friend who let the couple [Brandon and his new girlfriend] stay at her [house] said recently that, while she heard them arguing at about 3*

a.m., she went back to bed a short time later and didn't wake up until 7:30 a.m., when Brandon called from the restaurant where Stanton worked.... Newman said she could not provide an alibi for Brandon that morning. "I cannot say that he didn't leave my house at 3:30 a.m.," she said. "I don't know. I went back to bed."

The times were at variance to what she had told the investigators in 1990. Now, she confirmed a crucial gap of a few hours on the potential movements of Brandon. The story also noted that Brandon had broken into the Dare County Courthouse in the early 2000s.

Since the killing, Brandon has twice been charged and once convicted of breaking into the Dare County courthouse and trying to gain access to the vault where evidence from criminal cases is held.

Prosecutors suggested Brandon may have been looking for drugs. His son would later confirm that in an interview with podcaster Delia D'Ambra, saying his father told him he was high and drugs were his target. But some of Cliff's supporters said Brandon was seeking to destroy evidence held in the Spencer file that might be used against him.

—⁂—

IN A NOVEMBER 7, 2005 letter to Mumma, Cliff wrote about his assault convictions while in the service in Germany.

The reason for this letter is not to defend or apologize for not discussing with you about how sorry a man I actually was. I am by no means proud of the person I was when I was in the military. My reluctance to discuss in detail with you about my prior record probably has more to do with shame than anything else. I actually tried to block all this out of my mind.... That has been over 20 years ago and I have never discussed with my family how miserable an S.O.B. I was. I did not like myself at that time. Yes, I was into heavy drug use at that time, but other people use drugs and never acted like I did. There is no excuse for my previous actions and for me not talking to you about them, you did ask me on different occasions about my past and I never talked to you about it. If you had never read about my past in the S.B.I. file I would never have spoken to you about it. The reason for me not talking about it was not because I thought the police did not know, because it was part of the record, and I also knew that Mr. Murphy had a copy of my military record and I believe there was a copy of it in Judge Barnes' file. It was part of the discovery evidence....

What you read in the military report is accurate to what I did and I admitted to it. Yes I did assault two females, yes I was accused of 2 different sexual assaults. I was married for almost 10 years and I never assaulted my ex-wife....I once told you my past wasn't pretty. Now you know [what a] miserable person I once was.

—⚏—

STACEY'S FAMILY FOLLOWED THE probe of Stacey's death from New Jersey. One of their friends, retired Northfield police captain Randy Clark, repeatedly called Manteo officials, trying to keep up with the case, but answers were elusive.

17

FREEDOM AND ITS AFTERMATH

I really don't want to think they could have been that evil to go for me simply because I'm a Black man. But I'm not the first Black man to be wrongly convicted and I won't be the last. It flipped my world upside down.
—*Cliff Spencer in a March 2023 interview with the author*

On July 20, 2007, Cliff was paroled. He believes that the parole commission had finally taken into account the letter district attorney Parrish had written to it three years before, as well as a parole hearing in which Chris Mumma, Cliff and his parents testified. He had been locked up for seventeen years, counting the time he had spent behind bars before he entered his plea, but the state could have held him for life. Cliff's father picked him at the Currituck County prison unit, the latest prison to which he'd been assigned. The father hugged the son he had never given up on.

Stacey's mother, Maryanne Stanton, died the next year, on August 6, in her Northfield home. She was just seventy-six. She had never gotten over Stacey's murder. And she never relented, her family said, in her belief that Mike Brandon killed her daughter and Cliff was innocent.

In August 2010, Brandon was back in Manteo, dying of hepatitis C and cirrhosis of the liver. He had taken to calling himself by his given name, "Norman," in an apparent attempt at rehabilitation. He and his son had renewed their relationship, and the son was living in Manteo and often visited his father. The son, who was with his father when he died, said his father told him earlier, in effect, that he didn't kill Stacey, the son told podcaster Delia D'Ambra in August 2023. Brandon died at fifty-three on August 16, 2010.

Romallus Murphy, Cliff's initial attorney, died on December 21, 2011, at eighty-three. In a tribute to Murphy published in the *News & Record* newspaper of Greensboro, one of the nation's most effective and brilliant civil rights warriors, the widely admired Reverend William Barber, then the president of the North Carolina NAACP and a native of Cliff's northeastern part of the state, thanked God for Murphy's "meaningful accomplishments…that have improved the lives of many people across North Carolina and this nation."

Cliff found the tribute hard to believe.

Former Manteo police chief Steve Day died on July 27, 2013, in Elizabeth City at the age of seventy.

Frank Parrish, the district attorney whose letter stood up for Cliff at his parole hearing, died on September 22, 2013, at his Elizabeth City home at the age of sixty-four. His widow, Kim Parrish, told the author that "Frank was very humble, and I was not always aware of his good works. However, he always said that he would rather see 10 guilty men go free than one innocent man go to prison. I can assure you that knowing this [Cliff's case] was going on in the same office where he worked had to be very upsetting to him."

Stacey's father died two years later, on September 3, 2015. Just as his late wife, he never got over Stacey's loss, and talked lovingly of her until his last days.

Mike Brandon's sister, Tina, died on February 4, 2017, in her home in the Currituck County town of Aydlett. Her death came twenty-seven years and one day after Stacey's slaying. Tina, who discovered Stacey's body, had worked for food services for the Currituck County Public Schools system and driven a bus for them. She was sixty-one.

Joni Newman, who had recanted her alibi for Mike Brandon, died from injuries she sustained in a car wreck in Currituck County on October 6, 2021. She was sixty. Her ashes were scattered at the south side of Jennette's Pier in Nags Head, where Stacey had loved to beach-sit.

Superior court judge Herbert Small, who presided over Cliff's sentencing hearing, died in his Elizabeth City home on February 23, 2022, at the age of ninety-six.

—∽—

IN 2010, MUMMA HAD SENT a detailed request to the North Carolina Innocence Inquiry Commission, asking that it review Cliff's case. Six years later, without public comment or providing any information regarding their investigation, the commission staff declined to present Cliff's case to the commission panel and closed his case.

Unjustly, the records of this state agency are private unless it finds merit for claims of innocence in the last stages of its process and ends with a unanimous vote for innocence by a three-judge panel, an incredibly high burden to meet.

—⁂—

ON MARCH 7, 2023, I talked by phone with Murphy's associate on Cliff's case, David Dansby, at his Greensboro office, which he once shared with Murphy. Dansby was an old-school civil-rights warrior.

Dansby, then eighty-three, emphasized that Murphy brought him into the case late, shortly before Cliff entered his plea.

Dansby told me: "I don't want to besmirch him, but Murphy's personality was like a lot of lawyers. He did not like to try cases. He'd rather make a deal. I am a fighter. Mr. Murphy's personality was far different from that. He was in control of that one [Cliff's case]. It was his case."

He wasn't surprised that Murphy never interviewed any witnesses, he said. "I don't want to trash Murphy. I just want to clear things up so young lawyers will know to defend cases that need to be defended and won't be so anxious to get a plea. It's a lot of lawyers that want to take the easy way out." Dansby died in January 2024.

In April 2023, one of the SBI investigators refused to answer my questions on the case. He was sure Cliff was the killer, he said. When I asked him to explain why he thought that, he hung up on me.

In January 2024, Mumma told the author she was "looking at developments in DNA testing that might allow for further testing on evidence from Stacey's apartment."

The most recent DNA testing on that evidence was in 2016 by Bode Technology of Lorton, Virginia. It was on hairs found on Stacey's body and excluded Cliff and Patty Rowe, Mumma said. But because those tests were partial profiles, in which the full DNA is not produced, she said, the results were inconclusive on Mike Brandon. "Today's testing can pick up more DNA," she said.

She said in 2024 that she reviewed testing options with a forensic scientist from Bode and confirmed with the SBI lab that the DNA profile obtained

Above: The boxed and enveloped evidence in Stacey's case, shown to the author in July 2023 by the Dare County Sheriff's Office and held at its office in Manteo. *John Railey.*

Opposite: Envelope containing evidence in Stacey's case. *John Railey.*

from the green washcloth with bloodstains found outside Stacey's apartment is still being run through the DNA database. The best option for retesting is the paper towel with bloodstains found in Stacey's kitchen, she said, and she planned to contact the Dare County DA's Office to see if they will consent to retesting.

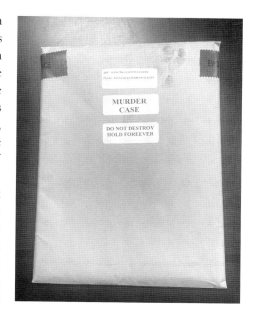

In July 2023, Dare County district attorney Jeff Cruden supplied the author with a list of more than forty pieces of evidence still held at the Dare County Sheriff's Office in Stacey's case, including hairs from Stacey's body. The author viewed the evidence, neatly packaged in boxes, manila envelopes and small cellophane bags. The potential for testing on the evidence is encouraging.

—⁂—

CLIFF HAD EASED HIS way back into the outside world, working blue-collar jobs, first living in Columbia and then afar. He met a medical student from South Africa who was studying in the nearby Tidewater region of Virginia. He married her and lived with her for a time in South Africa. He grew homesick, divorced and came back to North Carolina alone.

He became a long-distance truck driver, working long hours. In his late sixties, with many of his contemporaries retired, Cliff, lacking the savings to retire, keeps driving. He is bitter about the time the state unjustly robbed him of. Yet he's also realistic and says he wouldn't have been wrongly convicted if he had not been doing crack.

Cliff told me about that and many other things when I reached out to him in early 2022. We'd chat on the phone as he rolled across the South, the chronological time since his release ebbing but the mental pain since it always flowing. I told him why I was drawn to his story.

I'm a bit of a mystic. Stacey's body was found on my birthday, February 3. Her apartment was on the same street where Brenda Joyce Holland, the Manteo murder victim of 1967, had lived during her time in the island town. I wrote a book that came out in 2021 that sought to solve Brenda's unsolved murder journalistically, since the criminal justice system had failed her. I'd long been haunted by her story and that of Stacey.

In 1992, I had written a story for a true crime magazine about Cliff's case. I regret that effort, which I did to make ends meet as a small-time newspaper reporter. I based the story on law-enforcement sources and newspaper clippings and, in the pro–law enforcement style of such magazines, did not reach out to Cliff or his attorney. I worried about the story as I followed the media accounts of Cliff's case. I came to realize he had been wrongly convicted.

I realized that some power higher than me was pointing me to Stacey's case. I told Cliff that I had written the magazine story and wanted to make things right by writing a book about what really happened to him.

Cliff was driving as I told him I wrote that story. There was a long pause. Then he told me that my magazine story had angered him in his prison cell. And it had helped lead him to file his motion for appropriate relief. In a 2004 letter to attorney Chris Mumma, Cliff had written:

> *The details of Stacey's murder weren't pretty and it made me sick reading that story, that story would make anyone feel nothing but contempt for the person that thought so little of life. I shut down 3 or 4 months after that, "but" when I decided to try and do something about it the story made me angry.*

At that point, Cliff began writing his MAR. Cliff told me he appreciated my honesty. We began our shared journey.

We arranged to meet in person on Christmas Eve 2022 in Cliff's hometown of Columbia. That was a gift from Cliff, as returning to Columbia still makes him uncomfortable. Case nightmares. He doesn't go to the Outer Banks at all. But he graciously agreed to meet me in Columbia that Christmas Eve at noon.

I was working on the Outer Banks and left an hour early to make sure I could meet Cliff on time. The weather had been horrendous, Sound flooding the day before back in Kitty Hawk Woods where I was working from and freezing temperatures on Christmas Eve. We just roll with such weather on the Outer Banks. But when I got to the drawbridge over the Alligator River from Dare County to Tyrrell County and its county seat of Columbia, that old bridge on US 64 had frozen in the open position, and it was uncertain when it would open.

I cursed, turned my old pickup truck around and backtracked to the alternative route, up US 264. I called Cliff and let him know I would be late.

Cliff Spencer on Christmas Eve 2022 in the parking lot of the Tyrrell County jail, where SBI agents, without a legally required court order from a judge, loaded him into a car to transport him to neighboring Dare County for more questioning. *John Railey.*

Cliff Spencer in Columbia, North Carolina, on Christmas Eve 2022. *John Railey.*

No problem, he said. I raced down 264, a spooky road through swamps that runs by a U.S. Air Force bombing range and two cool old fishing villages, Stumpy Point and Engelhard, thinking much of the time about good and evil and Cliff's journey.

Cliff met me in Columbia. There is a certain easy gentle dignity about him, as well as a calm confidence. He is world-weary but still good. He took me on a walking tour of Columbia, showing me the jail where he was held and the sheriff's office where he was questioned, both part of an old brick building near Columbia's downtown. It is a peaceful-seeming structure, betraying nothing of the injustice that occurred against Cliff within its walls. There is a parking lot behind the building. Cliff stood in that lot for a moment, somberly describing to me his fear when the investigators took him out of the cell that night and led him to a car for the ride to Manteo.

"I really don't want to think they could have been that evil to go for me simply because I'm a Black man," he said. "But I'm not the first Black man to be wrongly convicted and I won't be the last. It flipped my world upside down."

As we continued our walk, Cliff occasionally stopped to talk to longtime friends who still live in Columbia. It was clear in that town, just as I'd found through interviews in Manteo, that many locals, Black and white, believe that Cliff is innocent in Stacey's slaying and that he was railroaded by defense attorney Murphy, district attorney H.P. Williams and the investigators. In the months ahead, Cliff and I developed a friendship as I worked with him and Chris Mumma to make a case, through this book, for Cliff's exoneration. At one point in the spring of 2023, Cliff happened to call me as I was trying to track down a witness. Cliff told me to be careful and that he would be watching his cellphone if I got in trouble. There was no danger, just a man sitting on his porch who was reluctant to help. I called Cliff and put him on speaker phone to try to persuade the man to help. Cliff made a good argument to the man. We got nowhere, but I like to think, from that moment on, Cliff and I have had each other's backs. Cliff keeps telling me to be careful, that we're both older now.

The criminal justice system failed Cliff. The chapter that follows is my theory on who killed Stacey and why, based on months of reading the case files, interviewing surviving insiders on the case, a career reporting on murder cases and, in the past few years, investigating mitigation factors in death penalty cases for the State of North Carolina. If future DNA testing proves me wrong, I will gladly apologize.

18

THIS CASE MADE STRAIGHT

I said my, my, my, I'm once bitten, twice shy babe
My, my, my, I'm once bitten, twice shy baby
—From one of Stacey's favorite songs, "Once Bitten, Twice Shy," sung by
the band Great White

Manteo, Saturday, February 3, 1990, early morning hours. The end to a pivotal week for Norman Judson "Mike" Brandon Jr. and his new girlfriend, Patty Rowe, culminating in months of buildup to a trigger that was about to be pulled. Brandon had threatened two women in the months before with a knife. He had talked negatively about Blacks, calling them "n———."

On Tuesday of that week, Brandon had sex with Stacey at the apartment they had recently shared. Rowe may well have heard about that, given that a few of her friends knew, and there are few secrets on the island. What is known is that Rowe found out on Thursday that she was pregnant by Brandon, and Stacey soon learned that, too. Friday night at the Green Dolphin, that backdrop became a hot mess, with Brandon, Rowe and Stacey colliding. Rowe was furious at Brandon, and Stacey wanted him back.

On his brief walk from the Green Dolphin Friday night, Brandon may have gone to Stacey's apartment, quietly opened the door and gotten furious at the sight of her lying on her mattress with a Black man, Cliff, but left before they realized he was there.

When Rowe and Brandon went back to Joni Newman's apartment, they argued about Rowe's pregnancy and what she saw as Brandon's continued attraction to Stacey. Around 3:30 a.m. on Saturday, Brandon slipped out of the house, walking to Stacey's apartment, one street over.

He opened the storm door through the hole in it and found Stacey alone, still awake and vulnerable on two counts: She loved Brandon, and she was intoxicated.

Brandon still cared for Stacey, but his emotions were surging. He quietly picked up a box-cutter knife from Stacey's kitchen counter **and slid it into one of his jean pockets**. He pulled on a pair of his work gloves he'd left there, joking to Stacey that his hands were cold. He started to make out with her, both of them standing near her mattress in the living room. Brandon rolled Stacey's shirt up. He pulled off his shirt and undershirt. Then anger overtook him.

Several weeks before, he'd broken up the fight between Stacey and Patty, but that had not ended things. Now, drunk and coked out, with his new girlfriend pregnant and Stacey wanting him back, he was done with the drama. He had said he wasn't on crack that night, but other sources indicated he was.

Brandon pulled the knife and cut away at Stacey's throat, all the fury with which he'd threatened women coming to fruition. Stacey fought back, but at five feet, five inches tall and 116 pounds, she was no match for Brandon, who was six feet, three inches tall and weighed 185 pounds.

They fell to the floor, half on the mattress. As Stacey struggled against him, Brandon pulled her sweatpants and panties off and pounded the inside of her left thigh with his free hand, the one not holding the knife, causing the bruising the pathologist found on the inside of that thigh.

As Stacey was dying or dead from her throat wound, he cut her right breast and vagina.

Brandon then went to the bathroom, using a gloved hand to turn the spigot on, then removed both gloves, washed his hands and cut the spigot off with his elbow so as not to leave fingerprints.

Brandon then peeled off his bloody pants and put on fresh ones that he'd left in the apartment from when he was living there. He put his shirt and undershirt, which were not bloodstained, back on. He quietly left the apartment and walked the block over to Joni Newman's house, dumping the knife, the gloves and his bloody jeans along the way. At Newman's, he returned to the couch.

Brandon had disposed of the evidence that would have tied the crime to him, including the gloves, which had protected him from leaving fingerprints on Stacey's body, although fingerprints on a body are notoriously hard to find. Being an experienced confidential informant, adept at working lawmen, Brandon then pinned the killing on Cliff.

District attorney H.P. Williams had initially resisted the investigators' push to charge Cliff. What caused him to change his mind? One of his assistants told the author in May 2023 that the turning point was Williams realizing, from what he was hearing from the investigators, that Cliff's description of Stacey's body was exactly how Agent Honeycutt had found the body as he processed the crime scene. Cliff told the author in July 2023 that he never gave that description to investigators.

Joni Newman later withdrew her alibi for Brandon, saying she couldn't cover him for the time around 3:30 a.m. until dawn. Patty Rowe had backed that alibi, but in her second interview with the SBI, she revised key statements she'd made about the timing of Brandon's movements early Saturday morning. Rowe had also said that, when she woke up after dawn Saturday, Brandon was wearing the same clothes he had on the night before. She may well have feared Brandon, a theory that's supported by court records of his later abuse of her and her own statements to the author. In addition, Brandon was known to wear blue jeans most days, so it would have been easy for her to miss him having changed his jeans.

The investigators clearly bungled the case. What is certain, what should have been certain from the March 1990 SBI test findings of no "Negroid" hairs on Stacey's body, is that Clifford Eugene Spencer did not kill Stacey Stanton.

Think about that testing for a minute. It wasn't just the wrong done to Spencer, as bad as it was. It was the wrong done to public safety in general: there were hairs on Stacey's body, not from Spencer, but from her killer. The SBI clearly chose not to find out to whom those hairs belonged.

So…

1. No physical evidence tied Cliff to the crime scene, except for his fingerprints that he admitted leaving when he visited in the apartment. DNA testing of hairs found on Stacey's body excluded Cliff. No blood was found on the clothes he wore around the time Stacey was killed.
2. Cliff never signed any of the statements attributed to him, nor did he admit to the killing in those statements.
3. He was taken illegally from the Tyrrell County jail to Dare County for the February 8 interrogation.
4. For many of the statements he allegedly made, his consent was questionable.

5. The murder weapon was never found.
6. Jailhouse informants did not incriminate Cliff.
7. Joni Newman recanted her alibi for Brandon.
8. The crime scene was compromised by numerous civilian bystanders trampling through.

The investigators may have gotten "tunnel vision," a dangerous and common malady to this day, an inability to consider other suspects once investigators develop an initial theory. The decision of the SBI not to order more testing that might have implicated a white suspect, while going for a Black suspect whose hairs weren't on the body, strongly gives the perception of a racist feeling on the part of the investigators.

District attorney Frank Parrish realized the problems in the case when he wrote his letter to the state parole commission in 2004. He should have reopened the case. But the fact that the commission took three more years to parole Cliff does not take away from the courage Parrish took in writing the letter and the commission's ultimate decision to parole him.

The author, seated far left, meets with Ed Stanton Jr., across from him, in Ed Stanton's home in Stacey's hometown of Northfield, New Jersey, in April 2023. Retired police officer Randy Clark is on Railey's left. *Kathleen Railey.*

Top: The author, seated far right, during the Northfield meeting, Meg Horton is seated across from him, and Sharon Stanton is standing. Ed Stanton Jr. is behind the author. *Kathleen Railey.*

Bottom: During the Northfield meeting, Stacey's friends and family celebrated her life. In the front row, left to right, are Elisa Jo Eagan, Sharon Stanton and Meg Horton. Ed Stanton Jr. stands behind Meg. On the mantelpiece behind Elisa Jo is a photo of Stacey's parents. *Kathleen Railey.*

Cliff's exoneration is long overdue, especially if new DNA testing further clears him.

It's encouraging that Stacey's family wants that as well. On a rainy afternoon on the last day of April 2023 at Ed Stanton Jr.'s house in Northfield, Ed, his wife, Sharon, and several other family members and friends welcomed my wife and me with good food and stories of Stacey. I told them she should be there with us. She *is* right here with us, they said, always.

In a later interview, one of Stacey's cousins, Cathy Groves, said, "We grew up in era where we really believed we'd find our Prince Charming and he would love us forever. It's like Stacey's dream was destroyed by this toxic nightmare. I got married, I had kids, I have a home. My cousin didn't get that, and she deserved it. It's just so wrong."

Ed Stanton said Stacey's cat, Molly, lived with him for several years until she died. "That cat absolutely knew what happened to my sister," he said.

Epilogue

Back to the source in the prologue of this story. She was Mike Brandon's girlfriend when Stacey was killed. Her name then was Patty Rowe. For several years after Stacey was killed, she was married to Brandon. Now she is Patty Moore.

Chris Mumma, Cliff's lawyer, and I visited Moore on a cool evening in April 2023 on the front porch of the house in the southern Piedmont of North Carolina where she was serving as a caretaker for an elderly couple. Moore was guarded but gradually opened up a bit, sharing what she said she could remember of the night Stacey was killed.

She remembered going, with Brandon, to Joni Newman's house on Devon Street in Manteo with Mike's sister, Tina, and a male friend of Tina's, the latter two soon leaving. Moore acknowledged, as noted in the SBI interviews, that Joni heard her and Brandon arguing at 11:45 p.m. and then at 5:30 a.m. She said Brandon was with her at Joni's until daybreak. But her son told podcaster Delia D'Ambra in August 2023 that his mother told him his father was out that night until the next morning.

In our interview, Moore would not say whether or not she thought Brandon killed Stacey. She indicated she would not have put it past him. "I didn't have anything against Stacey, beyond the situation with Mike," she said.

She acknowledged that she and Stacey fought over Brandon in the parking lot of Stacey's apartment a few weeks before Stacey was killed and that she had found out she was pregnant the week before the slaying.

After she left Brandon because of his assaults on her and divorced him in 1997, Moore said, she heard nothing from him. He eventually left the island. So did she.

When I told Cliff about the interview, he said he was glad to hear that Moore was talking about the case.

Many Outer Bankers believe Cliff is innocent. That includes some locals who harbor their own prejudices in general about race.

One local told me that Brandon never being charged "ate me up for a long time because I know damned well he did it." That local had served time with Cliff at the Gates County prison. "He seemed to be an all-right dude," the man said of Cliff. "I never thought he had anything to do with Stacey's killing. But you got one man in jail…you kind of leave it alone because there's nothing you can do about it."

Outer Bankers keep Stacey's legacy alive. One, Jessica Duffy, lived in Stacey's apartment several years after the slaying. Changes to flooring and a wall had been made, she said, to erase the bloodstains. "I always thought what happened to her was so wrong," Duffy said, "and I hope justice can be served in her case."

Cliff has tried to make the most of his life since his release from prison. He talks frequently with his daughter. Before his father, Harry Spencer, died several years ago, he told Cliff he was proud of him. That warmed Cliff's heart.

In 2023, Cliff's mother, who'd stood by him throughout his fight, was in a nursing home in Elizabeth City, North Carolina. Cliff could see she wasn't getting the care she needed, she wasn't eating, so he paid out of his limited funds to have a certified nursing assistant work with his mother a couple of hours a day to make sure she ate. "All those years I was in prison," Cliff said, "she sent me twenty dollars every two weeks for the prison canteen. Helping her is the least I can do."

His mother died in April 2023. Cliff drove to Columbia for the funeral, hugged his family and friends and drove back to his Georgia home the same day. "I just don't care to be up there," he said, saying that what happened to him in Columbia and Dare County in 1990 still makes him uneasy.

He occasionally talks to Judge Edgar Barnes. Barnes told me recently that he really wanted to win Cliff a trial. He, or any decent lawyer, for that matter, could have won Cliff an acquittal, given the state's weak evidence, he said. "It would have been a heck of a trial," he said.

Cliff stays in touch with Mumma, sharing with her the dream that they will one day persuade the State of North Carolina to exonerate him.

It would be nice to end this story with Cliff riding down the road in his Mack truck. Conventional wisdom says the road sets you free. But at sixty-seven, Cliff is hurting, driving for a living past the retirement many of his peers enjoy. He and Stacey are frozen forever on February 3, 1990, always with the ghosts from that winter Friday night, the quick and the dead, on the island.

In the interview, I asked Patty Moore why she had fallen in love with Mike Brandon. "I don't know. It was all so long ago," she said with a sad laugh, her eyes still as blue as those waters from the winter of 1990.

A hawk soared nearby, looking for weakness in some small creature far below.

Acknowledgements

My thanks to all the sources, named and anonymous, who helped me bring this book together. Some case insiders declined to be interviewed. Others bravely helped. Roanoke Island friends ushered this Nags Head boy once again through the complexities of their sand. We're all Dare County, separated by the narrow Roanoke Sound, but the island has its own private culture.

Through three nonfiction books set on the island now, I am honored to say I have gained some islanders' trust. Thanks to islanders Angel Khoury for a great edit, Claudia Harrington, Harrell Lee Bundy, Donetta Livesay, Beulah Ashby, Wayne Morris, Nancy Austin, Bernie Austin, Joann Selby, Carlton Walker, Yoyo Daniels and Earlene Sawyer. John Wilson IV generously updated his fine Manteo map to show key sites on the case.

Nancy Lamb, who was a prosecutor initially involved in the case, gave wise counsel. Dare County sheriff Doug Doughtie, as always, provided solid help.

The best lawyers on the case, Edgar Barnes and Chris Mumma, patiently answered my many questions. Sonya Pfeiffer, when she was a University of North Carolina law school student under Mumma at the North Carolina Center on Actual Innocence, wrote a powerful case summary.

Delia D'Ambra, who grew up in Manteo, produced a good podcast on the case on *CounterClock* in 2020 that greatly renewed interest in the case, and she generously shared insights and contacts.

Thanks to Outer Bankers Buddy Tillett, Jessica Duffy, Debra Johnson, Jimmy Ray Watts and Elton Ray Griggs. My longtime buddy McMullan Pruden also provided keen insight.

Once again, the fine photojournalist Drew Wilson generously allowed me to use his photos.

Stuart Parks of the Outer Banks History Center, supported by tax dollars and donations, supplied, as always, solid help.

In Kitty Hawk, Inga Eglitis Francis gave me my second home, as always. Inga and her husband, Rick, are both lawyers, and they supplied me with wonderful insight as we discussed the case. Nothing's better than writing on their back deck in the moonlight, their rescue boxer, Kelly, often by my side.

My sisters, Jo Beall and Mimi Merritt, and Mimi's husband, Rob, inspired my storytelling, as did my daughter, Molly, and Freddy Hampton and the rest of our Outer Banks family.

Stacey's brother, Ed Stanton, and his wife, Sharon, were instrumental in welcoming my wife and me to South Jersey and depicting the times in which Stacey was raised there, as were her cousins Meg Stanton, Cathy Groves and Mary Powers. Elisa Jo Eagan and Randy Clark also provided needed assistance from Stacey's hometown. My sister-in-law Susan Rossi and her husband, Sal, graciously gave my wife and me lodging in their house for the Jersey journey.

Thanks to my friends at Arcadia Publishing, Kate Jenkins, Abigail Fleming and Jonny Foster, and to my friends Mary Giunca and Cam Choiniere. Mary gave the manuscript a good edit, and Cam formatted it.

Once again, Sam & Omie's restaurant and bar in Nags Head, my shrine, provided me with a fun spot to connect with sources. Cheers to Carole Sykes and her hardworking team. At Lagerheads Tavern at Wrightsville Beach, North Carolina, owner Jim Carter and his main man Mark Ellington provided solid encouragement.

As always, my bride, Kathleen, was instrumental.

A salute to my big brother, attorney Richard Railey Jr., who gave me learned counsel on this book. He died unexpectedly on the July 4, 2023 holiday at his Kill Devil Hills cottage with family. He was the best, always standing up for the highest standards in his murder cases and all the rest of his work. I see you up there in the Outer Banks stars, brother.

Most important, thanks to Cliff Spencer for trusting me with his story.

Bibliography

In writing this book, I drew from the SBI file, defense attorney Chris Mumma's case file, records from Dare County Superior Court, the transcript from Cliff's plea hearing, his motion for appropriate relief (MAR), transcripts from his two MAR hearings in Dare County Superior Court, meeting minutes from the Manteo Board of Commissioners, hundreds of my own interviews and stories published in the *Coastland Times*, the *Virginian-Pilot* and the *News & Observer* of Raleigh.

I reached out in 2023, either in person or through intermediaries, to the key investigators on the case. They declined to be interviewed. Manteo police chief Steve Day had died a decade before.

The SBI declined to comment. Brad Eilert, the Manteo police chief, said in a January 2024 phone call that his department has no plans to reopen the case due to its age.

Cliff said the SBI interviews quoted him out of context after leading questions and were often just dead-wrong. I tracked down as many of the people interviewed by the SBI as I could to check the accuracy of their statements. I found many problems in the SBI interviews, both in commission and omission, which I note in the book.

Tackling the work of Romallus Murphy on Cliff's case was hard. His civil rights work will stand, but he did fail Cliff, just as we can all fail in our endeavors.

These books were immensely helpful, including three of my own:

Gaw, Amy Pollard. *Lost Restaurants of the Outer Banks and Their Recipes*. Charleston, SC: Arcadia Publishing, 2019.

Gray, R. Wayne, and Nancy Beach. *Manteo*. Charleston, SC: Arcadia Publishing, 2020.

Khoury, Angel Ellis. *Manteo: A Roanoke Island Town*. Virginia Beach, VA: Donning Company/Publishers, 1999.

Railey, John. *Andy Griffith's Manteo: His Real Mayberry*. Charleston, SC: Arcadia Publishing, 2022.

———. *The Lost Colony Murder on the Outer Banks: Seeking Justice for Brenda Joyce Holland*. Charleston, SC: Arcadia Publishing, 2021.

———. *Rage to Redemption in the Sterilization Age: A Confrontation with American Genocide*. Eugene, OR: Cascade Books, 2015.

Visit us at
www.historypress.com

About the Author

John Railey has spent much of his life on the Outer Banks. His previous books from The History Press, *Andy Griffith's Manteo: His Real Mayberry* (2022) and *The Lost Colony Murder on the Outer Banks: Seeking Justice for Brenda Joyce Holland* (2021), have been top sellers on the Banks. A graduate of the University of North Carolina at Chapel Hill, he is the former editorial page editor of the *Winston-Salem Journal* and investigates mitigating factors in death penalty cases for the State of North Carolina. He has won numerous national, regional and state awards for his writing and investigative reporting. He is also the author of the memoir *Rage to Redemption in the Sterilization Age: A Confrontation with American Genocide.*